P

This is the book that cult le

It gives the game away; reve
mystical curtain of deception.

The book places the reader into the mindset of a would-be cult leader, inherently highlighting the techniques of control and manipulation that are used by unscrupulous people to use and abuse unsuspecting members of the public. **Come to think of it, politicians might not be happy about this book either.**

It doesn't, however, take into consideration the concerns and feelings that cult sufferers and their Loved Ones have; it can't because of its satirical structure. There are some fascinating books that do this – '*Beyond Belief*' by Jenna Miscavige Hill, '*Escape*' by Carolyn Jessop, '*Unfollow*' by Megan Phelps-Roper, and also '*Underground*' by Haruki Murakami, to name but a few.

No. This book jumps with both feet, squarely into the mind of a psychopath, who has learnt through trial and error, how to get what he wants from people.

A word of warning: it's a very unpleasant place to be. Given that a cult leader is self-centred, pompous and deeply insecure, it is no surprise to learn that most of them are men! It therefore means that the journey ahead is driven by cutting cynicism, testosterone-filled aggression, and the darkest of human desires. **Sorry!**

If this all sounds way too scary and unsavoury (or too raw because you have lost a Loved One to a cult), you are welcome to 'cheat' and jump to '**The One Real Truth**' on **page 183** to see if you want to get on this Roller Coaster… It's up to you.

Sit back, fasten your seatbelt, and brace yourself for a rough ride through the trials and tribulations of the world of a cult leader.

Good luck!

First published in 2022

The authors would like to thank the various sources, including Rex/Shutterstock, for the use of the photographs in this book. All photographs retain their original copyright status. The authors apologise for any unintentional errors or omissions, that will be corrected in future editions of this book.

Front cover image designed by Richard Francis © 2022, and created by Trev Penn.

Back cover photograph by Sean Buckley © 2022

A catalogue record for this book is available from the British Library.

ISBN: 978-1-7396826-6-8

Printed and bound by CPI London (UK),
38 Ballards Lane, Finchley, London N3 2BJ

WAY OF THE MASTER

How to create a Cult in 6 easy Stages

Table of Contents

FOR RON...

THE MASTER OF MASTERS

A Personal Message

Would you like to have wealth and riches beyond your wildest dreams? Maybe you want to roll around naked in piles of cash, laughing loudly as other people endlessly toil away, providing you with all of that money.

Or, would you like to have your over-blown ego massaged by devout worshippers who hang on your every word? Maybe you want the kind of power over people that allows you to command anything without resistance and have them thank you for the privilege of serving you.

Talking of 'massages', perhaps you would like to have access to young, nubile attractive women (or men) who will satisfy your deepest, darkest desires? Maybe you want to use tantric exercises to get your sticky, filthy fingers on their smooth, firm flesh.

Or, are you simply a sociopath who would get pleasure from destroying as many lives as possible whilst making a quick buck in the process?

If you've answered yes to any or all of these questions, then you have in your hand the 'Golden Ticket' to a journey of discovery that will lead you to a bright new future.

You will probably have already realized that just ordering people (or as I like to call them – minions) to worship you doesn't work, unless you are the head of a military regime… or Kim Jong-un! Not all of us can be that lucky, so you will have to fool people to get what you want – or as we say in the Cult Trade, you'll have to 'Deceive to Receive'. **If you are a decent, honest human being, don't bother trying to be a Cult Leader; you will fail. A Cult Leader must rid themselves of any morals or ethical tendencies that they may have accidently picked up through life; it will only get in the way.** If you are worried about deceiving people, and their reactions to you for that deception, then don't give it a second thought. **There are MANY people who WANT to be deceived**…

…as long as you promise them the kinds of things that I have laid out in this helpful and insightful book. As Machiavelli once wrote, "*…men are so simple, and prone to being won over by the necessity of the moment, that a deceiver will always find someone willing to be deceived.*" – 'The Prince'.

Niccolò Machiavelli wrote 'The Prince' in 1532 to Lorenzo de' Medici, Duke of Urbino, as a guide on how royalty can maintain power, but the advice can work just as well for Cult Leaders. So much so, that 'The Prince' is required reading for anyone who wants to understand what goes into Cult Leadership. Don't worry if you find reading a bit boring, as it is a short book and very easy to 'pick up and put down'; a lot like 'Way of the Master'.

How is this deception to be achieved? Contained within these glorious pages are the Steps and Stages, Levels and Phases that you will need to go through to make your dreams a reality.

'Way of the Master' is all you need to understand why and how people join and remain inside a cult.

And there is no better time for starting a cult than now. Collectively, our civilization is in bad shape, slowly but inevitably sliding towards terminal destruction from environmental degradation, economic depression, and natural resource depletion. All of which will lead to a reduced quality of life for the vast majority of the human population on this damaged, dying planet… **What a fantastic situation to be in!** As the world reels from one crisis to another, and as the traditional main-stream faith organizations can no longer conceal the level of corruption and abuse that is going on within their own walls, hundreds of millions of people, scared out of their wits, will search for alternative belief systems out of desperation and abject fear. **Remember, fear is the greatest catalyst for control that there is… ask any politician.**

This is where you come in. As an emerging entrepreneurial 'Master', you'll be perfectly positioned to capitalize on what's predicted to be massive growth in the cult business sector in the coming years, ONLY… only if you are willing to take my advice.

I am certain, without doubt, that you'll find this book both enjoyable and greatly instrumental to your success as you learn what it takes to run a cult, dominating and controlling others (Please see Stage 1: Step 2: Always be Certain). I have the unique skillsets and knowledge to provide this vital information. I am the ONLY author who 'tells it as it is' (Please see Stage 1: Step 4: Be the 'One and Only').

Whatever you do, however, DON'T show this book to your minions (or anyone else for that matter). If people find out about the tricks and techniques that I discuss in this book, it will become nigh-on impossible to fool them into joining a cult.

KEEP THIS BOOK A SECRET!

So, if you are ready to take the first Steps to the new You…

…take a deep breath and turn the page.

Welcome to the rest of your wonderful life.

Welcome to… The Way of the Master.

Professor R L Francis

Stage One:

Finding Your Inner Master

"A man's gotta make at least one bet a day, else he could be walking around lucky and not even know it."

Jim Jones, Suicidal Leader of The Peoples Temple

Ever heard this saying?

> **Q**: What is the same, no matter where you go?
> **A**: YOU!

Well, you're about to read one of the most profound statements in the history of mankind, and it is an absolute factual truth…

YOU… are the key… to a successful… YOU!

Wow, right? The cult that is created; the minions who will follow; the society that will condemn, *ALL* of it will be driven by your personal character. At its core, *a cult is a sociological construct, which serves as an apparatus to elevate a single personality over, and at the expense of, the other members, by using psychological and physiological techniques of control.*

That 'single personality', dear reader, will be YOU.

This may seem very daunting. Can a normal 'Joe' really become the divine prophet that so many people need in their small and insignificant lives? Can a 'Zero become a Hero' so easily?

No. Of course not. Don't be stupid. YOU are one of those people who have a small and insignificant life; that's why you want to be a Cult Leader, right? But, if you follow my unique, simple **6**-Step Program, **you will *appear* to be the Leader that everyone would want you to be, and that is enough for most people**.

Every journey starts with the first step. You may be thinking to yourself – "*I haven't got the right credentials or achieved any life accomplishments to make people put their trust in me.*" Perhaps you're worried about not being handsome or charismatic enough to charm people into submission, or that your imperfect past will hold you back from being seen as something special.

Don't worry. Most of the world's successful Cult Leaders have been heavily flawed, downright selfish, rotten to the core, pig-ugly, talentless, vile and corrupt excuses for human beings. That is until they re-invented themselves with a Transformational Epiphany…

STEP 1: Have a Transformational Epiphany

"It happened one day when I was riding on a school bus, gazing out of the window. I had a vision of a whirlpool pattern and I just knew that the flow of energy I was seeing was the same in an atom, as in our entire solar system. I felt deeply that I too was somehow made of that same pattern."

Foster Gamble, Leader of the Thrive Movement

This step comes in many forms. Sometimes it's a cosmic experience, sometimes it's a journey of discovery or a self-imposed period of exile (don't worry if you hate travelling, it can just be a 'spiritual journey'), and sometimes it's simply a mystic revelation. In each variation, the transformational epiphany serves as a metaphorical metamorphic mechanism, changing one from a mild-mannered regular fellow into a God-like figure of divinity.

For the minions that you'll someday lead, the Transformational Epiphany will become part of your cult's folklore/narrative; a cue that you, the Cult Leader, are something exceptional. It provides a reason for your minions to both trust and follow you.

> *Why should your minions follow you?*
> **Because you are the chosen one who was foretold by prophecy!**
> *Who created and spoke of this prophecy?*
> **You did!**
> *How can your minions know that you are telling the truth?*
> **Because you are the chosen one who was foretold by prophecy!**

It's perfect circular logic, which is the best sort of logic to use when dealing with minions. For the aspiring Cult Leader, the Transformational Epiphany is useful because it allows him the freedom to 'cast off' his past mistakes and wrong-doings and become re-born as a powerful and commanding Cult Leader.

The beauty of this step is that being a pathetic excuse for a human being prior to the transformation only increases the legitimacy of the epiphany, as if to say, *"This experience was so powerful, it was able to transform that wretched human into a divine being worthy of worship"*. How fantastic is that?

Shoko Asahara

As an example, consider the case of Shoko Asahara who was the leader of the Japanese cult Aum Shinrikyo.

Short, fat, ugly, talentless and nearly blind! Despite these vast shortcomings, he was able to create a cult that had over 10,000 minions, with millions of dollars in the bank, and an international influence. Yes, that 'influence' did include multiple attacks on civilians, such as the infamous Tokyo Metro sarin attack in 1995, but it's an influence nonetheless!

Born Chizuo Matsumoto, Asahara lost his normal income when he was convicted of selling fake medicine back in 1981. To make up for this loss, he tried to create a cult a few years later but failed – if only this incredible book had been around to help him, right? He then said that he went on a pilgrimage across the Himalayas (even though there is no evidence of this), and came back a changed man. Well, he had grown a beard and long hair, learnt a bit of yoga, and had 'discovered' that he was both the re-incarnation of the Hindu god Shiva AND the Egyptian architect, Imhotep; hey, if you're going to make this stuff up, you might as well have fun with it!

He changed his name to Shoko Asahara and developed amazing mystical powers like levitation and walking through walls… although this is questionable given that he was held in prison for several decades and then executed by hanging in 2018!

Prophet Raël

Then there's Claude Maurice Marcel Vorilhon, otherwise known as Prophet Raël of the space-age sex cult, Raëlism.

Vorilhon was a struggling racing car journalist for his own magazine in France in the early 1970's. That all changed in December of 1973, when he took a bicycle ride into the French countryside and was abducted by a UFO; don't you just hate it when that happens? Inside the spaceship, he met Jesus, the Buddha, and the Elohim, who were an alien race that gave him special abilities.

When he returned to planet Earth from a quick tour of the cosmos, he was instantly reborn as the Prophet Raël, who foretold of a date that the aliens would return and render judgement onto the people of Earth. This judgement would be based upon read-outs of a supercomputer, which was calculating the moral value of each individual person… or something like that – the Raëlian mythology has had numerous changes over the years!

Stewart Traill

The creator of the Church of Bible Understanding (COBU) was just a simple vacuum machine repairman… until God endowed him with a true interpretation of the Bible, all the previous ones having been wrong, of course! He would attain thousands of followers and amass millions of dollars.

A couple of other Cult Leaders worth mentioning are -

David Koresh, who was a failed rock musician, upon joining the Branch Davidians in Waco, Texas, had the revelation that, in fact, he was Jesus Christ reincarnated.

Alan John Miller, who was a failed Jehovah's Witness preacher, whilst detained in a mental institute, had the revelation that, in fact, he was Jesus Christ reincarnated.

Joseph Smith

But by far, one of the most successful examples of the Transformational Epiphany is that of Joseph Smith, the creator of Mormonism.

Joseph Smith was wandering around upstate New York in the late 1810's, promising to find gold with a divining rod for a fee to any unsuspecting victim. He was actually in a lot of trouble with many unhappy customers who wanted their money back, but then he was 'visited' by an Angel called Moroni and shown two golden tablets. Joseph Smith hadn't kept the tablets, of course, but he promised that they existed… which was good enough for his followers!

The rest, as they, is history. But Joseph Smith took this technique to a new level with the recurring or Perpetual Transformational Epiphany (PTE), this is to say that Joseph Smith repeatedly had messages directly from God… whenever he needed them, really. For instance, when his wife caught him having an affair, he had a Transformational Epiphany that God intended for him to take multiple wives. Nice! Joseph's concept of ongoing epiphanies was so successful that it became a foundation of the Mormon ideology known as 'Divine Revelation'. To this day, Mormonism is rife with breakaway splinter groups precisely because of so many leaders claiming to have experienced a divine revelation to the one truth, such as Ervil LeBaron and his Church of the Lamb of God.

A word of warning! '*With great power comes great responsibility*', and this technique can be abused far more than it should be by any respectable Cult Leader. For example, I don't recommend the direction that Ron and Dan Lafferty took in their Fundamentalist Mormon cult, School of the Prophets. As told in the book 'Under the Banner of Heaven', the Lafferty Brothers received divine instruction to murder their family members who had argued with them. After the brothers had gone on a killing spree, they blamed it on God. **This isn't the sort of Transformational Epiphany that you should adopt, as blaming mass murder on a divine god has a way of putting people off!**

While the form of the epiphany changes, the purpose is always the same – a moment, act, experience or understanding that demarcates the old self from the new, and serves as the point of re-birth and transformation into a worthy idol.

Your Transformational Epiphany will work best if it coincides with a physical change in your appearance; growing a beard or a moustache is said to convey authority; wearing white or blue clothing subliminally represents purity and confidence. Playing dress up like this helps with your performance and goes a long way towards '**Personality Projection**'. It would also be helpful to change your name; most of them do it. You can change it to mean something important, like Mun Yong-Myeong did when he created the Unification Church and called himself Sun Myong Moon, which means 'the word made clear'. As did Chizuo Matsumoto, when he chose Shoko Asahara, which means 'Prosperous Fields'. Or you can just play with it. Orville T. Gordon, who created the Outer Dimensional Forces, simply reversed his surname and called himself Nodrog. Or you can just steal names from other sources like Claude Vorilhon did when he chose 'Raël' and then said that it meant '*Messenger of the Elohim*'... honest, it does!!

My favourite, however, is when Chandra Mohan Jain, after changing his name numerous times, finally went down the pop star route by using a single word – 'Osho' by Calvin Klein! How Rock Star is that?

All of this leads to a simple, comforting conclusion for aspiring Cult Leaders everywhere; **It's quite all right if you're not the person that you will someday *say* that you are**.

Take a few years off and prepare yourself; cults aren't built overnight, you know. Randomly berate and chastise people on public transport. Take acting or hypnosis classes. Memorize small portions of the Bible and then pretend that you know all of it. Get into theological arguments with street preachers; it is so easy to get a reaction out of them! Really play around with your experiences. Then, and only then, will you be able to say that you've had an organic, natural and completely fake Transformational Epiphany. **Then, and only then, will you become reborn with the one and only Truth… whichever truth you've just made up**.

But, the most important advice regarding the Transformational Epiphany is that you must show absolute conviction when recounting your story. Never, under any circumstances, waver or show doubt about the power of your fabricated transformation. It's important that you are certain about this fake event. If you don't believe in your own transformation, how can you expect anyone else to believe in it… which leads us neatly to the second step…

STEP 2: Always be Certain

"I can say, with absolute certainty that Marshall Applewhite was a second coming of Jesus and I know it's true."

Rio DiAngelo, sole survivor of the Heaven's Gate mass suicide in 1997

The second characteristic that all Cult Leaders need to possess is a steady, constant, and undying sense of certainty in all situations, even when they are obviously wrong and everyone in the room knows it. This may seem counter-intuitive but there is method in the madness.

Let's look at an example from another system of social deception and delusion – Politics! Despite obvious mental vacuity for much of his presidency, George W. Bush retained largely popular approval ratings in public opinion polls. In fact, it took two failed wars and the near destruction of the global economy for the American people to finally decide that maybe they weren't that enamored with him, after all.

President Bush maintained this popularity mainly from the simple technique of being seen to be decisive. He made decisions quickly, and with great certainty, even when he was obviously factually and ethically wrong. On the campaign trail, Bush often called himself, 'The Decider'.

Leadership surety isn't simply a recommendation, but rather a necessity proven through scientific research. Many psychological studies have shown that people can be afraid of change and uncertainty, and they respond to certainty because it's the one thing they don't have in their own lives. In his 2008 scientific paper, David Rock identifies 'Certainty' as a key factor in influencing people's behavior – 'SCARF: A Brain-Based Model for Collaborating with and Influencing Others.' He describes the process like this – "*A sense of uncertainty about the future generates a strong threat or 'alert' response in your limbic system. Your brain detects something is wrong, and your ability to focus on other issues diminishes. Your brain doesn't like uncertainty –*

it's like a type of pain, something to be avoided. Certainty on the other hand feels rewarding, and we tend to steer toward it, even when it might be better for us to remain uncertain."

Most studies have concluded that the brain develops a virtual version of the world around us so that it can form a 'shorthand' process when dealing with it. Instead of having to rediscover how things work each time, which is energy consuming, the brain makes assumptions and predictions from the virtual version and acts upon them. When these predictions are correct, all is well, but when things don't match, there is a conflict within the brain that research has shown induces a feeling that is similar to that of the stress caused by physical pain[1]. The brain, therefore, seeks out certainty and tends to avoid ambiguity. Fortunately for Cult Leaders, the brain extends this natural neurological process far beyond its capabilities into socio-political and economic predictions, which are impossible to accurately forecast, yet the brain still gravitates towards claims of certainty. You can take advantage of this flaw by feeding the desire.

Human beings pretend to want careful deliberation from people in authority, but this often results in nuanced choices and complicated outcomes, which can be confusing and disconcerting. So, the opposite is actually true. Studies have shown that, contrary to what they say, people would prefer to follow a decisive leader even when he's wrong more often than not, than a cautious leader who gets it right most of the time (*Harvard, CEO Genome Study*).

The fact is that you certainly need to be certain about being certain, that is for sure!

All of which is to say that, as a Cult Leader, when you say or do something, even when you're obviously wrong, or coming out with utter nonsensical gibberish, do it with complete conviction and your minions will nod and pretend to understand what you mean.

---

[1] Although this IS based on actual research (Eisenberger, Lieberman UCLA), don't be afraid to use phrases like 'studies have shown' or 'research proves' even when it isn't true, as this will lend credence to your claim and most people won't bother checking out the facts. **Lying is a necessity for being a Cult Leader.**

This is the joy of surety; you don't have to make sense for people to agree with you.

If you are telling your minions that the end of the world is coming, don't allow for any nuance or room for error. Don't *suggest* that you *think* the end of the world is coming, or that you *suspect* that the end of the world *might* be near. NO! The end of the world IS coming. You are CERTAIN of it. There is not a DOUBT in your mind. Along with giving your minions the mistaken idea that you actually know what you are talking about, absolute certainties also feed into the false 'black and white' Binary Landscape narrative that you'll be developing for your minions. I'll detail this more in Stage 2: Part 5: Motivational Mythology, Page **6**5.

One common mistake that many aspiring Cult Leaders make is to assume that if they are certain about a decision that turns out to be wrong, they will be remembered for this error; that this record of bad decisions will be held against them. These poor naïve fools have clearly not heard of **Confirmation Bias**, where people only remember the events that support their view of the world and conveniently forget the times when their position was contradicted. As long as you have followed my advice and done your job properly, your minions will only remember the odd occasion that you get things right and ignore all of the other times when you have royally screwed things up. **Many politicians owe their entire careers to Confirmation Bias!**

> A study in 2009 at the Ohio State University showed that people spent nearly 40% more time looking at information that confirmed their political stance than on the opposing position. This number can greatly increase with how 'personal' the issue is and how it affects the reader directly. Food for thought!

The lesson is simple: When people see or hear you get something wrong, follow the three D's – *DENY, DENY, DENY*, and let Confirmation Bias do the rest.

It's quite all right and even, dare I say it, proper for Cult Leaders to rewrite history for their minions by asserting that true things are untrue and untrue things are true, perhaps using the phrase 'Fake News' whenever they want to muddy the waters. In fact, as a Cult Leader, it's your duty to confuse your minions into thinking that they are certain about which they have no certainty of, as this triggers a flawed cognitive process called the **Dunning-Kruger Effect**. This is when people with substantial, measurable deficits in their knowledge, memory or expertise lack the ability to recognize and assess those deficits and, therefore, despite potentially making error after error, tend to think they are performing competently when they are not. **In other words, a Cult Leader must ensure that his minions are so ignorant about how to understand things, that they become too ignorant to understand how ignorant they are!** Again, many politicians benefit from this flaw, particularly Presidents, but if you want to get a really good idea of how this works, study the 'Flat-Earth Movement' or the Moon Landing conspiracies and you will see the Dunning-Kruger Effect all over the place!

As well as screwing with the minds of your minions, this practice will 'rally the troupes' by turning the 'Fake News' into an attack on you and your group. I will detail this very useful technique later in Stage 5: Lesson 1: Persecution Principle: Page 137, but for now, if the flawed thought processes haven't really kicked in yet, it is important to use a simpler version of the Persecution Principle within your own cult by creating a socially sensitive environment, whereby minions who still have some clarity in their minds will feel pressured into not saying anything about your numerous mistakes. Minions should feel like they cannot question or challenge anything you say or do, and that they will be ostracized from the group if they do; Peer pressure is a very useful tool of control.

But is this true? Can this dynamic work in the real world?

Let's find out from a factual, real event...

Case of a real Anecdotal Account

In the late 1990's, a student of mine – I'll call him 'Joe', started a cult in rural New Mexico where he convinced all of his minions to abandon their Earthly possessions to a trust that was owned by one of Joe's corporate entities (Text-book move, nice!) Unfortunately, on several occasions, Joe contradicted himself during sermons on the reason for the minions to give up all that they owned. On one occasion, Joe stated that it was because God despised wealth. On another occasion, Joe stated that it was because God valued wealth and wanted to see if his followers would be willing to sacrifice such an important commodity; to see if they were worthy of being the chosen ones. (Both positions will manipulate people but it's not wise to use them on the same minions at the same time!)

Generally, this discrepancy went unnoticed, but on one occasion, a new minion raised his hand and asked about the contradiction. As Joe had been making this stuff up as he was going along, he was taken a bit off guard. But instead of debating with this minion or attempting to justify himself, Joe remembered my instructions and immediately belittled the minion in front of the group and shamed him. This particular man who interrupted Joe happened to be impotent and had previously felt that he was unable to please his wife, a secret he had shared with Joe in his 'Private Counselling' (**Always get to know the darkest secrets of your minions**). So, of course, it was this that was used against him, publicly revealing his secret to the others. "*How dare you, a man who cannot even please his wife, challenge me, the Son of God!*", Joe thundered. The minion immediately went red with shame and fell silent. The others also quickly got the message and, despite the numerous contradictions that riddled his daily teachings, Joe was never again interrupted while in the middle of a sermon. [2]

[2] This is a completely fabricated anecdotal account but it's ok to make them up, most people don't check. Even if it was a real event, most anecdotal accounts are so unreliable that they might as well be fictional. So, have fun with making up stories that 'prove' the truth of your claim.

The lesson to be learned from this 'true story' about Joe's past is that you can't engage in debate or discussion with your minions. You cannot admit to your errors and put your minions on an equal footing, no matter how egregious or obvious your errors are. **Treating minions like this simply elevates them to respectable, decent human beings and a Cult Leader should never do that?** The only reasonable response to someone who publicly notes your contradictions is to attack; *DENY, DENY, DENY – ATTACK, ATTACK, ATTACK.* Repeat when necessary.

Your minions MUST see you as the sole arbiter of The Truth for them to feel justified in following you. Being absolutely certain about your position, and stamping out any dissent within the group, will go a long way to achieve this. As Chris Johnston said in the documentary, 'Holy Hell' (2016), when he was describing his time in the cult, Buddhafield[3], "*The only truth that's left is the truth that I am told. And who is the highest authority in the group? It's the Master.*" Well said, Chris. You knew your place!

Important Update:

In the digital era, and with video cameras in people's smart phones, your statements will invariably be recorded and viewed on websites like YouTube or public news channels and can easily be discredited – **most cults control what minions view, or even order them to avoid technology altogether, particularly the Internet, to solve this problem** (and I go into how to deal with these media issues in more detail on page 140 – Lesson 2: Media Management). This potential access to information and facts may seem like a disaster, particularly if Peer Pressure hasn't taken a hold yet, but fear not. The third step towards becoming a Cult Leader will take care of this danger by utilizing a cognitive flaw that occurs in most people…

---

[3] Buddhafield was created by James Gomez back in the 1980's. He changed his name to Andreas, then Michel, then Rostand… mainly to avoid the claims of sexual abuse by the male minions.

STEP 3: Embrace Hypocrisy

"Every one of you girls who spreads out your arms and your legs on the bed for those men are just like Jesus, exactly like Jesus!"

David Berg, Cult Leader of Children of God

Cult Leaders must have the ability to openly revel in double standards without any pangs of guilt. You must be able to moralize about the sanctity of the human body whilst sexually abusing anyone you can get your dirty hands on. You must be able to keep a straight face when you condemn the evils of capitalism whilst you stride, proudly, onto your own private jet. You must be able to advocate respect and equality whilst abusing your minions and treating them like slaves.

This process is exemplified in George Orwell's Dystopian novel '1984', with the corrupt government's slogan being "WAR IS PEACE, FREEDOM IS SLAVERY, IGNORANCE IS STRENGTH." This book is another 'must read' for anyone wanting to understand what it takes to be a Cult Leader.

This serves two main purposes.

Firstly, it allows you to attain and enjoy whatever your heart desires, as **it is easy to get from people that which they think is bad for them**. If you want money, just proclaim that money is the root of all evil and that your cult can save followers by taking it from them and turning it into goodness… mainly by spending it on yourself. If you want adulation, then instruct your minions that the selfish human ego negates any chance of salvation… and they must worship you to rid themselves of that destructive personality flaw.

This may seem counter-intuitive; how can people not see the obvious contradictions in these positions? Trust me… they don't!

So much so, that Osho's minions raised the money themselves to buy 93 Rolls Royce limousines for him to enjoy (They were his favourite vehicle!), at the same time as he was 'teaching' them about the harm of consumerism and capitalism. He actually got his minions to line up on the road to wave to him as he drove by, going towards their lessons. Brilliant!

Their plan was to buy him 365 Rolls Royce's, one for every day of the year, but the plan came to a grinding halt when he was thrown out of America for illegal activity!

Stewart Traill convinced his minions that they needed to get a couple of private planes for him to travel around quicker, spreading the virtues of austerity and abstinence. It also helped him to take many of his female minions on private 'joy' rides.

The second advantage to living a hypocritical life is that it compounds the thought-stopping processes that your minions will be going through (Discussed later in Stage 3: Phase 4: Page 96), as they will have no choice but to operate **Cognitive Dissonance** in order to accept the contradictions in front of them. You could say that it is your duty, as a Cult Leader, to live a hypocritically privileged life for the sake of your minion's salvation… you could say that… even if it is a complete pile of doggy doo!!

As Machiavelli puts it in 'The Prince' – "*...although a Prince need not have all the good qualities that I have mentioned, it is most necessary for him to appear to have them. I will even be so bold as to say that it actually does a Prince harm to have those good qualities and always observe them. But appearing to have them will benefit him.*" Wise words, Niccolò, wise words indeed.

This double think can be exploited in so many ways that it is worth spending a few moments discussing the phenomena and seeing how it is used to control and abuse people.

Cognitive Dissonance is when a person holds two or more opposing ideas in their mind at the same time. It is a form of personal mental deception that allows humans to accept the discrepancy between what they want the world to be like and how the world really is. It allows, for example, someone to order a diet soda, telling themselves that they are healthy, whilst tucking into a double cheeseburger with extra bacon and onion rings… proving that they are anything but.

In psychological terms, people like balance and order (consonance) and when there is something that disturbs that equilibrium, they will perform mental gymnastics to at least give the appearance of harmony (Festinger, 1957).

Usually, as most people have little control over the Outside World, this entails twisting the importance of an emotional or ethical value that they themselves hold. For example, when a child is abused by a parent, the victim will often blame themselves for the crime, saying that they deserved it in some way rather than accepting that their parent could do wrong (Lichtenberg, 1994). This is exactly the same dynamic that you should be enabling in your minions. As you will be seen as special, particularly as a father-figure, the privileged or abusive behavior will be justified in some way, usually by seeing it as for the betterment of the group or as an uncomfortable but necessary step towards salvation.

The minion's thought process should go like this –

"*As my Master is so special, it is only right that He should live a different and privileged lifestyle to us. I know that He is so special because He shows us the true, correct way to live our lives.*"

By joining Cognitive Dissonance with Circular Logic, you will have created a mind-numbing loop that should last a lifetime.

A very simple technique to heighten the use of Cognitive Dissonance in your minions is to give contradictory instructions.

For example, Stewart Traill came up with the catchy slogan, 'Get Smart Get Saved', which he put on badges and posters. This was at the same time that he was forcing his minions to give up on their education to work for free in his cleaning company.

David Berg told his college student dropouts in California that they didn't need to follow any oppressive rules, man!... except for the ones that he was enforcing.

Sun Myung Moon, having bought a Lamborghini for one of his sons, lectured to his Moonies about living a virtuous, simple life before, during and after he got out of prison for fraud… with his minions paying for the fines!

My favourite though, is when Osho gave his 10 Commandments, which described the absolute truth that his minions had to follow, one of which was – "*Truth is within you, do not search for it elsewhere*." Awesome! This really screws with their minds.

Hopefully by now, you will see how important it is for Cult Leaders to embrace hypocrisy; ALL of them do it. It is an integral part of what allows them to live a privileged life; why else would someone want to be a Cult Leader. **What is the point of your minions seeing you as something special if you can't exploit it?**

So, don't be afraid and enjoy it.

Talking of being seen as something special… the next step is one of the easiest, as you, like all Cult Leaders, are narcissistic and already see yourself as something special! The tricky bit is to convince others of this. Onto Step 4.

STEP 4: Be the 'One and Only'

"The True Buddha is born as only one man, in one religion and in one age, there is only one who can teach the highest Truth for all the people."

Ryuho Okawa, Cult Leader of Happy Science

A Cult Leader must be seen as the ONLY person who can guide people towards salvation; your minions must think that you are the only option that they have for success. It may seem obvious that, as there are thousands of Cult Leaders out there, the chances that someone has found the 'One True' Leader is remote… or even impossible given that we are all making this stuff up, right? Luckily for you, people don't think like that. Most people are biased towards a **Jackpot Mentality** where they are confident that, against the odds, they have found the one person who can lead them to eternal bliss.

If people were being sensible, they would try and find a decent balance in their lives, learning from many words of advice by different philosophers and teachers; reading many different books rather than just one… but when has sensibility ever been the main stay for most people?

Use this flawed thinking to your advantage by explaining that, without ABSOLUTE devotion to you, the minions will NOT reach salvation. This puts you into an incredibly powerful position.

Obviously, bringing 'The Truth' to your minions will help them see you in this light, and the aforementioned Transformational Epiphany will also add weight to your 'specialness', but I can let you in on a great trick that you can have up your sleeve.

Claim that you have Extra-Sensory Perception (ESP)!

That's right! Appear to have the ability to know things about your minions that you couldn't have known. Don't worry. You don't actually have to have this gift… who does? It's known as **Cold Reading** and it's easy to get the hang of it.

There are several different ways of operating it. One way is to throw out some generic phrases that could apply to most people and then let the minions do all the work, fitting what you've said to their personal experiences. This is called **The Barnum Effect**. Say things like "*You are a very kind person but you do recognize that there are times when you can be selfish*" or "*Your wisdom is gained from life experiences rather than just book learning*" or, and this is a great one, - "*You like to be in control but there are times when you really feel insecure*" ... who couldn't identify with that one? If you want to get familiar with this kind of language then read some **horoscopes**, as they use this technique all the time!

Another version is when you use questions that can easily be turned into 'statements of fact' once the minion has answered them. For example, "*Are you satisfied with your career or is there a problem?*", and if they say that they're ok then you can nod and agree, but if they say 'no' then you can nod and say "*I thought you looked lost.*" Another question can be, "*What is it about your health that concerns you?*" - most people are concerned about their health! If they tell you what's wrong then you can nod and say "*I sensed that about you.*", or if they feel ok, you can suggest that they look a bit peaky and that they should eat better – most people could eat better!

Even if you get a 'miss' now and again, our old friend **Confirmation Bias** will make your minions forget those times and remember the occasions when you appeared to be 'spot on'.

Hey Presto! You have ESP!

If you would like to become an expert at this technique, then I would recommend Ian Rowland's 'The Full Facts Book of Cold Reading'. If this, however, all seems like too much hard work then there is a much simpler secret that I can reveal to you.

Give yourself a False Title of Importance!

"*Seriously, Professor?*", I hear you cry. Yep, this sounds too simple to be effective, but it really works; most Cult Leaders do it. Jim Jones called himself 'Reverend' even though he was never ordained or had any formal training. L. Ron Hubbard considered himself a doctor, even though he had dropped out of university.

Joseph Di Mambro proclaimed himself as '*The Cosmic Master*'… I don't even know what that is, let alone how to qualify for it!

The point is that if you make your minions automatically use titles or superlatives when they talk to you, or about you, then, subconsciously, your special status will be legitimized.

This title will also reinforce and continually serve as a reminder of the transformation that you have undergone – you used to be a nickel-and-dime financial advisor in a large corporation in Japan, but now, after your epiphany, you are 'El Cantare', the re-incarnation of the God of Gods… as in the case of 'Master' Ryuho Okawa and his Happy Science cult.

Along with having immense power over your minions, another valuable reason for why you should be seen as 'The One and Only' is to avoid falling into a very dangerous trap, a trap that stems from the fact that you are doing all of this for an easy life. It can be tempting to 'share the load' of running a busy cult with someone who will be seen as your equal. Resist this temptation, as it will inevitably lead to a conflict of interest and a disastrous power struggle, fatally ending your cult and possibly even your life.

Joseph Di Mambro

Joseph Di Mambro had several failed attempts at running a cult in the 70's, but then, in the early 80's, he met Luc Jouret who was a doctor, practicing in another industry that uses subterfuge and deception – **Homeopathy**. They joined forces and changed Mambro's ailing cult 'The Golden Way' into the 'Order of the Solar Temple' in 1984. Things improved for several years with increased membership, real estate, and money laundering. Millions were made but jealousy and paranoia soon set in.

Mambro, the self-proclaimed '*Cosmic Master*', declared that his daughter, Emmanuelle, was the new messiah, as she had been conceived without the act of sex (or at least that's what his wife had told him!) This was a slight problem as Jouret had declared that he himself was the third re-incarnation of Jesus Christ (There's a lot of Christs in the world, aren't there?) and therefore superseded her. Tensions grew as Jouret developed a science fiction angle to the cult but Mambro wanted to retain the religious theme.

More doubts set in over Mambro's abilities to contact higher powers (presumably because he didn't have any) and there were whisperings about internal corruption. The final straw was when a couple of minions, who were loyal to Jouret, had a baby boy called Emmanuel. This was seen by the paranoid Mambro as a direct challenge to his daughter's authority. In September of 1994, he ordered their deaths under the guise of the boy being the Anti-Christ, and this triggered a violent implosion. Within a week, most of the core members, including Mambro and Jouret, were found dead in a ritualized killing spree. Most had been murdered, including the two leaders, with only a few being genuine suicides. It all ended up being a very messy affair largely due to the conflict of interest between two Cult Leaders.

Rajneeshpuram Movement

It can also be tempting to let a high-ranking trustee take charge of your cult whilst you spend your time enjoying yourself. After all, that's why you want to be a Cult Leader, right?

Don't do it. This can be just as bad as having a second leader.

Osho made this mistake when he was in America in the 1980's. Osho's secretary, Ma Anand Sheela – otherwise known as Sheela Silverman, got her wealthy husband to buy a $6 million ranch in Oregon to use as their compound, where Osho could take drugs and have sex with his minions without interruption, and Sheela could rule the roost. Unfortunately, the novice soon lost control and the physical abuse, drug selling, and attempted murders exploded beyond 'acceptable limits' and there were attacks on people outside of the cult – a rookie mistake.

The authorities were brought in and Osho tried to deny all knowledge of the 'goings-on', which is a bit difficult to do when you are the boss of the same place where it is all happening… even if it is spread over 64,000 acres! He tried to avoid capture but was caught, fined $400,000 and thrown out of the country. Not good!

Bonnie and Marshall

The only cult worth noting that had a relatively successful partnership was Heaven's Gate (HG), which was formerly known as the Total Overcomers Anonymous (TOA), which was formerly known as the Human Individual Metamorphosis (HIM) – see what happens when you keep making this stuff up?

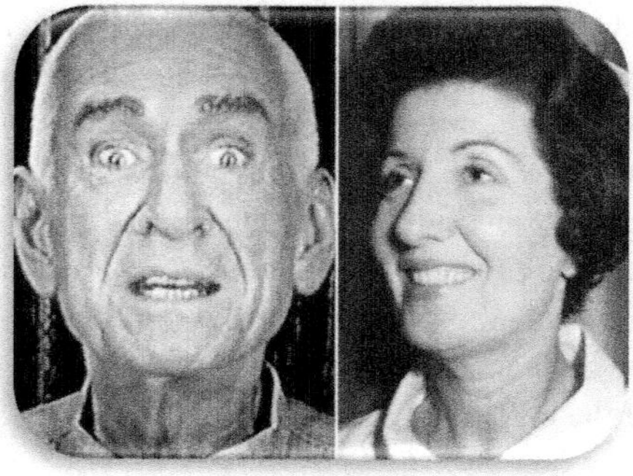

Marshall Herff Applewhite and Bonnie Nettles first met back in the early 70's when Bonnie was a nurse in a Mental Institute and Herff was, let's just say… visiting for a while!

In the cult, Marshall, who had changed his name to Do but also went by the names Tiddly, Ningen and Guinea… (don't ask!), took on the role of Messiah; and Bonnie, who had changed her name to Ti but also went by the names Peep, Wink, Pig, Poop and Shelly West… (seriously, don't ask!), took on the role of soothsayer.

As they both wanted adulation and received it in abundance, they were content with the dual dynamics. Their minions worshipped both of them equally as two supreme, perfect beings who were destined to lead the faithful up onto a spaceship to salvation…

…that is until Bonnie went and selfishly spoilt it all by developing cancer and dying in 1985!

This inevitably changed the dynamics of the cult and things gradually spiraled out of control. Marshall became progressively isolated and even though he pretended that he was getting messages from Bonnie saying that he was the 'Only One' to follow, the writing was on the wall. Knowing that his reign was coming to an end, and whilst he still had the last remnants of control over his minions, he took the arrival of the comet Hale-Bopp in 1997 as a sign and ordered them all to 'disembark' to the great spaceship in the sky. 39 people, including Marshall, died in his suicide pact. Very sad! What a waste of all that effort to change and control people! So, even a supposed success like Heaven's Gate didn't really pan out as well as might be expected.

This doesn't mean that you must run the whole process on your own. To help with the momentum of your cult, you can employ a '**Supporting Witness**', otherwise known in sociological terms as the 'First Follower', highlighted by the entrepreneur Derek Sivers in 2010. This is someone who recognizes how special you are and acts accordingly, encouraging others to join you.

The Supporting Witness can be your most trusted minion, a spouse, or a best friend. Their role is very important; an enforcer of rules, assistant in the logistical planning of cult management, and most importantly, lubricating a crowd by being the first to clap or be amazed at your sloppy vague attempts at prophecy; stand-up comedians are known to put plants in their audiences who will laugh hysterically at their jokes. As we all know, compliance – like laughter – is contagious.

Derek Sivers describes it like this, "*Being a First Follower is an under-appreciated form of leadership. The First Follower transforms a lone nut into a Leader. If the Leader is flint, the First Follower is the spark that makes the fire. A movement must be public. Everyone needs to see the followers because new followers emulate followers – not the Leader.*"

Managing a cult is largely predicated on forms of social control, and many forms of social control are reliant upon techniques of peer pressure. Consequently, your Supporting Witness should be the first person to raise their hand and volunteer, the first person to bow at your feet, and the first person to suggest compliance.

Examples of successful Supporting Witnesses include Karen Zerby who 'persuaded' David Berg to fulfil his potential with his Family of Love, Hak Ja Han who was instrumental on 'forcing' Sun Myung Moon into a millionaire leadership role, and Credonia Mwerinde had 'shared' visions from the Virgin Mary with Joseph Kibwetere in the Movement for the Restoration of the Ten Commandments of God.

You can reward your Supporting Witness for their services, but you must resist the temptation to treat them as an equal. Remember, you MUST BE the 'One and Only'.

The best analogy to use is that of a Cult Leader being a sheep farmer, controlling his flock. When you only have a few sheep to control, you can do it yourself. If you intend to get more sheep than you can handle alone, then you get yourself some sheepdogs NOT more sheep farmers. These sheepdogs can think that they have some control, but they must still do everything that you tell them. You must never lose control.

You must be seen as THE ONE AND ONLY.

Of course, there is always a danger of your narcissistic desires for absolute obedience and control to be taken as arrogant and manipulative… because it is! This judgement might get in the way of your path to success, but don't worry. Step 5 will take care of this potential problem.

STEP 5: Project Humble Righteousness

"Some people see a great deal of God in my body. They see Christ in me, a hope of glory."

Jim Jones, Suicidal Cult Leader of the Peoples Temple

The fifth characteristic that all Cult Leaders must adopt is the ability to exhibit an insufferable righteousness – sometimes interchangeably referred to as piousness. As a Cult Leader, you should be drowning in an ever-present piety whether you are relaxing by the pool in luxurious comfort or having sexual relations with numerous wives of your minions.

For this piety to work without alienating the very people you want to abuse, it is vital for it be composed of two components: a razor-sharp moral outrage and an ever-present modest or reluctant narrative of regret and repentance.

The moral outrage serves as the angry voice of condemnation and judgement, aimed at the Outside World and any minion who doesn't do what they are told.

The reluctant narrative serves as a counter to the completely justifiable accusation of dictatorial dominance and narcissism by claiming that the Cult Leader regrets being in this position but must 'put up with it' for the betterment of others.

One component cannot succeed without the other. If you just show moral outrage all the time then you'll be seen as an arrogant, annoying prick and, likewise, if you just show a modest, reluctance all the time then you'll be seen as a whining, annoying prick. Combine them together, though, and you'll be seen as the **Saviour of Mankind**.

Moral Outrage

As a Cult Leader, you will be defining the sub-culture that you wish to build from opposition to the larger cultures in the Outside World. This opposition will be mainly constructed by creating a moral dichotomy between yourself and everyone else; a dichotomy supported by a good helping of really extreme outrage at all that you think is wrong with the world. You must be seen to have moral superiority to everyone else, especially to your minions so that they aspire to your levels of moral purity and perfection. But, because you are lying through your teeth, they will naturally fail to succeed in their aim, thus starting their cycle of guilt and self-recrimination.

Your moral outrage also gives you something to rail about in your never-ending lectures or sermons. It doesn't matter what you are outraged about, just as long as you are REALLY outraged about it. It can be drug abusers, sex offenders, politicians, liberals, greed, gluttony or just general 'bad stuff'. Let's face it. There's enough crap in the real world to rail against that you'll have plenty of ammunition to draw from.

A moral hierarchy should be constructed, where you are at the top, your minions below you, and the external Outside World below them – with the ever-present carrot of the minions being lifted to your dizzy heights, and the ever-present stick of the minions being sent down below. If you are feeling ambitious, you can create levels of moral worth within the cult itself, assigning your minions to these different levels, using designated titles of importance with a corresponding uniform to match, a bit like the armed forces (See Scientology). You can reward and punish them through the gaining and losing of those levels; nothing is more amusing than seeing those minions scramble to achieve some spiritual designation that you have entirely made up!

Warren Jeffs

One of the most pious Cult Leaders is Warren Jeffs, the now imprisoned leader of a sect of Fundamentalist Mormons. Consider the following quote made by Jeffs during his trial – "*You are now touching on what is sacred! I say to you, let it cease! This trial must cease if there is to be justice! I say to you, this is a court*

of unjust ways, not of justice! I say to you the government is stepping beyond these bounds!" It's worth noting that he was convicted of multiple charges of child rape and kidnapping. This is moral outrage at its most audacious.

Moral outrage is a trait that you, as an aspiring Cult Leader, must seek to replicate and master, although I would like to stress that it should be done **without sexually abusing children**.

Reluctant Narrative

To counter all of this outrage, the Modest or Reluctant Narrative is the process whereby a Cult Leader *unenthusiastically* takes on the privileges of his lofty position without wishing to do so… honestly! He really doesn't want to be the centre of attention or be thrust into a leadership role, but finds that, for the sake of others, it is *necessary* for him to do what needs to be done; after all, who would want to be a millionaire, being worshipped by hordes of devoted followers, right?

Most often, this terrible *ordeal* will have to be *endured* because a God has ordered the Cult Leader to follow the path, and who is he to say no to a God, or perhaps it's because the Cult Leader alone has discovered the One Truth that will bring peace and harmony to the world and is therefore *consumed* by a deeply felt personal responsibility, where he feels *compelled* to live out his destiny, even though he doesn't really want to… Can you smell it yet?

An extra twist on this position is to pretend that you didn't even know that you were something special, and use the Supporting Witness as the person who 'discovers' that you are the 'Saviour' – it worked for Bonnie Nettles and Marshall Applewhite… for a while, anyway… you know… until they all died!

You can almost hear your minions talk about you behind your back, discussing with each other your divinity – "*It must be true that He is the Chosen One because He doesn't want to do it. He's sacrificing His life for the rest of us against His own will. Who else would do that except for the Chosen One?*"

This is precisely the sort of twisted logic that you need to encourage in your minions.

For instance, when you're caught in a moment of wince-inducing self-promotion, while you're telling your minions that you alone, of all the people on the Earth, have the power to heal the planet, make sure you throw in a bit of Reluctant Narrative at the end with – "*Of course, I don't want to take on this position but neither do I want to let people down, so I have to fly in my private jet to save as many people as I can; it would be wrong not to do so!*"

Let's say you're in the midst of punishing your minions because they failed to obey one of your impossible demands on them. For example, perhaps they were supposed to have finished constructing a filter system for a Sarin gas factory that you are building to induce Armageddon (as in the case of Shoko Asahara and his Aum Shinrikyo cult) but because they hadn't slept for 30 hours, the minions had made mistakes and not completed it in time. When you punish them, do so reluctantly – "*I don't want to lock you in the cellar and leave you there for 3 days. In fact, it saddens me deeply to do so, but if you fail then the whole group fails, and we won't reach salvation. I have no choice but to chain you up!*"

That sort of crap!

But the Reluctant Narrative can also be used offensively! Instead of attributing your 'responsibilities' to a higher power or deeper calling, attribute it to your minions; it is they who have put you in this position. You are doing all of it for them. All the trials and tribulations that you will have to endure; the 5-star hotels, 7-course meals and sexual partner after sexual partner, all become the fault of the minions. This will make them feel incredibly guilty and, as any parent knows, guilt is an effective tool for inducing control and subservience. If you get it right, you will have your minions thanking you for making these 'sacrifices' for them, and they will apologize to you as you punish them. Very satisfying!

This may sound overtly cruel and nasty… because it is! But then again, cruelty is an essential part of being a Cult Leader… as you are about to find out by taking the final and most difficult step!

STEP 6: Make Cruelty Your Best Friend

"REPORTER: How much evil is inside you?
CHARLES MANSON: As much as you see.
REPORTER: How much do you see?
CHARLES MANSON: All of it!"

Exchange between Charles Manson and a reporter

To be a Cult Leader, you MUST be cruel. This may seem odious or uncomfortable, but it's something you have to accept as true. *You cannot develop a cult by treating your minions with respect!* (This is so important that it is worth repeating) *You cannot develop a cult by treating your minions with respect!* **If you are treating your minions with respect and as equals, then you don't have a cult, you have a group of nice friends... and where is the profit in that?**

Being respectful and supportive is antithetical to the very idea of being a Cult Leader as it hinders the success of reaching his goals. Obviously, your minions mustn't see you as cruel and nasty but there are techniques to blind them to that, which I will go into later. The fact is, though, you MUST see your minions as a means to an end; as stepping stones towards your happiness – being walked on whenever needed.

For this to work, a Cult Leader requires absolute devotion from his minions, and the best way – some would say the only way – to get this absolute devotion is through the use of cruelty.

The specific implementation of cruelty needs to follow a very simple pattern: Love - Cruelty – Love – Cruelty – Cruelty – Love, in alternating and repeating sequences. **This creates what is better known as Battered Spouse Syndrome (BSS)**, whereby the abused partner is trapped in a cycle of fear and guilt, as the abuser blames the partner for the cruelty but then shows remorse in, what's often referred as, the 'honeymoon period' after the cruelty. In most cases, it creates a form of Post-Traumatic Stress Disorder (PTSD) that lowers their self-esteem, stops them from reaching out for help from loved ones, and warps their understanding of what is real. **The perfect dynamic for a Cult Leader!**

Obviously, I am NOT advocating spousal abuse; it is a deeply immoral act and an offense to humanity. Abusing your minions, however, IS A NECESSITY!

LEGAL DISCLAIMER

This book, and all the related material, is a satirical critique of cultism, and of the human divisive tactics that people use to profit from others. Although we have referenced actual accounts from real cults throughout the book to provide valid warrants for our criticisms, we are in no way condoning or advocating these practices, and our work should NOT be taken literally.

Now that we have covered ourselves legally…

TORTURE YOUR MINIONS! TREAT THEM LIKE DIRT! DE-HUMANIZE AND BREAK THEM DOWN!

It may seem like a contradiction that a leader who is supposed to be helping and nurturing his followers is actually harming them… because it is, and you may wonder why the followers would put up with such behavior; how can they not see the cruelty around them? **Well, welcome back to our old friend Cognitive Dissonance!**

As in the case of children who have been abused by their loved ones, BSS victims will also try to 'find equilibrium' by fabricating any excuse for why their partner is behaving so badly, often blaming themselves for the abuse. They, in fact, begin to crave the 'honeymoon' periods and take the bad times as part of the deal, even if it's poisoning their lives.

Any Cult Leader worth their salt will push this dynamic to the max. His goal should be to have his minions praise him to the Outside World for being a tolerant, loving and nurturing leader, whilst being petrified to say or do anything wrong, wincing at any possible retribution from him. This really goes a long way to destroying the minions understanding of the Self, (Discussed later in Stage 3: Phase 5: Page 99).

Charles Manson

Charles Manson had a small but very devoted group of young minions who he turned into murderers that would kill on command. Manson was able to do this, in large part, by his alternating use of love and cruelty.

Patricia Krenwinkel came to Manson's ranch in the late 60's as a young woman, scared and alone in the world with a small child to care for. Manson first exhibited love and affection by taking them in and promising to provide for them in his desert hideaway; she instantly became part of the 'Family'. He also became Patricia's lover as she was so special to him (even though he became a lover to most of his female minions), and constantly praised her, writing a song about her as she was so special to him (even though he wrote a song about most of his female minions). This gave her badly bruised ego a much-needed lift.

But then, quite suddenly, Manson would turn violent, whipping her with a belt, and knocking her to the ground when she questioned his behavior. Then later, after the abuse, he would make love to her in that 'honeymoon period'. **His female minions craved his 'unconditional love' whilst trying not to break the conditions he'd set for them.** He would not have had so much control over them if he hadn't have done this, and history would be very different. As Krenwinkel described it herself, so succinctly – "*It is countless how many lives were shattered by the path of destruction that I was a part of, and it all comes from such a simple thing as just wanting to be loved.*" Too true, Patricia. Too true.

Cult Leaders are able to manage such spectacular obedience from their minions, not because they are simply cruel (any old sociopath can be constantly cruel) but because they are cruel WITH periods of affection and supposed love.

In fact, it is often this '**Coercive Kindness**' that can be used as a specific device to transition into the cruelty; directly blaming the victim for the abuse, compounding the guilt and low self-esteem.

Lafayette Ronald Hubbard

L Ron Hubbard is infamous for the cruelty he displayed to his Sea Org members who accompanied him on his sailing trips around the world while living in exile, avoiding criminal charges. It is said that Hubbard would make members walk the plank into the ocean, and lock them up in the engine room naked, forcing them to eat out of a slop bucket.

The punishments, as he explained to one of his minions after locking a deaf-mute girl in a locker for a week, was to raise their level of 'confront' in order to someday deal with the evil in the universe. This was Scientology techno-jargon, meaning that Hubbard was toughening them up to survive future space battles against the forces of Xenu, the evil intergalactic warlord; not unlike an angry and cruel Drill Sergeant, shaping recruits into strong soldiers, ready for war.

He didn't want to do all of these horrible things (remember to always use the Reluctant Narrative!) but they were necessary for their future survival. He was doing it for the sake of his minions! **The ultimate aim for a Cult leader is to get his minions to see cruelty and suffering as a virtue. Most people will endure anything as long as they believe it to be a test of their worthiness.**

A tough step, **only** if you are **not** a psychopath… but if you are not a psychopath, then why are you trying to become a Cult Leader?

Checklist for Stage 1

If you have followed my unique and easy-to-use **6**-step program, you should now be reading this book wearing a white robe, covered in a blue shawl, having grown a beard. You will be certain about how your fabricated Transformational Epiphany really did occur, and that you are the 'Only One' who has really had one; the rest of the so-called leaders being lying, manipulative and exploitative charlatans (Nudge, nudge, wink, wink!).

Your name should be Zargon, or such like, and you should have a superlative title like '**T**he **U**niversal **R**uler of **D**estiny' for people to call you, over and over again. Don't forget, you'll get called this a lot so make sure you are happy with it!

You should be ready to tell people how to live their lives, and be willing to be cruel to them so that they can achieve this; after all, you are just doing it for their sake, as you never wanted to be a multi-millionaire in the first place, right?

Sorted!

Now that you look and act the part, we need something for you to sell to the waiting public. You need a cult, which is Stage 2.

But before you move onwards, I want to see if you have really taken on board what I have taught you. I don't want to waste my precious words on someone who is not taking this seriously.

Take the test and let me see if you are worthy of moving onto the next stage.

End of Stage 1 Quiz

Answer the questions below and see how you have scored.

Question 1) How will you describe your Transformational Epiphany to future minions?

A) It was an incredible experience that has changed me forever.

B) It proved to me that I was the Chosen One to guide people to a better world.

C) These kinds of serendipitous events can be used as a positive motivation to improve our lives and inspire others.

Question 2) What would be your actions if someone questions a claim that you have made?

A) I would repeat my claim and then apply the Persecution Principle to suggest that they had ulterior motives.

B) I would embarrass them by using personal information that I have learnt from our 'Disclosure Sessions' to shut them up.

C) I would openly debate the issues that they had raised to encourage free thought and independence.

Question 3) Why would your minions accept the double standards within your behaviour?

A) Because a leader must be seen as different to his minions. It's an unfortunate necessity.

B) What double standards? I'm sacrificing my life for them!

C) Because they suffer from flawed thought processes like Cognitive Dissonance and Confirmation Bias that allows them to ignore reality in favour of a fantasy.

Question 4) How many Cult Leaders are in operation around the world?

A) There are many charlatans who say that they are a prophet, but I am the only one who can really be trusted. Honest!

B) One. Me! And don't you forget it!

C) At least 200,000.

Question 5) When should you apply the Reluctant Narrative?

A) On a regular basis to avoid the accusation of arrogance.

B) Whenever I want to abuse a minion… which is always!

C) Never. Misrepresenting yourself is wrong.

Question 6) Who would allow themselves to be subjected to continual cruelty?

A) A person who understands that there are sacrifices to be made if they want to reach salvation.

B) Any minion, if they know what is good for them!

C) A vulnerable person who has been subjected to repeated acts of mental and emotional manipulation.

How did you do?

Mostly A's – I bow down to a 'Master in the Making'.

Mostly B's – It's a good start, but you might want to rein in the rage a bit. Read Step **6** again to see how controlled cruelty is better.

Mostly C's – Yeah, I'm not sure you're really getting it. Open your mind, think things through thoroughly… and just accept whatever I am telling you… or else!

Stage Two:

Creating Your Reality

So far, I've shown you the Steps that you need to take to be seen as a great leader. I've taught you how to transform yourself through a fake epiphany… that really did happen, and I've explained the need to revel in 'reluctant' cruelty, certainty, and a good dose of hypocrisy.

But, so what? You're a lone person without anything to sell, and a Cult Leader without a cult is no better than a Reality TV celebrity! **It is the vehicle that the Cult Leader is driving that will make people want to get on board and be taken for a ride.**

So, on to Stage Two: Creating Your Reality.

Like a custom-made car, built to order, your cult should be designed from the bottom up, with parts chosen to compliment and support each other, resulting in a vehicle that satisfies your own desires and requirements; why make a two-seater electric car when you want to have a big family?

Luckily for you, I have created a **6**-Part template that will help you understand what goes into making a cult; an easy-to-follow self-assembly Instruction Manual, if you will. Some of the parts are simple to understand but others have greater complexity to them. **Don't be a typical male by ignoring the Instruction Manual and blindly striding on.** Take your time and actually read the instructions for once! Please take advantage of this unique opportunity. **Most Cult Leaders have had to learn about this process through trial and error but not you, dear reader**. You have it all laid out before you. Skim over this stage and you will fail, as many have done before you.

This may seem like a lot of work, particularly as you are doing this whole thing to have an easy life, but I can assure you that a little bit of effort in the short term will pay vast dividends in the long run. Think of it this way. If you were told that you could work hard for a couple of years and then relax for the rest of your life in luxury, you'd do it, right?

PART 1: Aim of your Cult

The first component of your vehicle is the aim or purpose of it. In other words, what is fueling your need for having a cult? Is it adulation, money, sex, power, or a mixture of these and more?

Why is the fuel or aim of the cult worth considering?

The sole purpose of a cult is to serve and satiate the Cult Leader.
(This is so important that it is worth repeating)
The sole purpose of a cult is to serve and satiate the Cult Leader.

As only a fool or a masochist would join and stay within such a selfish system, the cult must appear to support and help either all the minions within the cult, or the chosen few who will succeed within the cult, or the entire human race, nay, the entire universe... only if the minions do their job properly within the cult.
But, NEVER FORGET.

The sole purpose of a cult is to serve and satiate the Cult Leader.

It is important, therefore, to remember why the cult has been created. The subsequent choices you make for the engine, chassis, seat capacity, etc., will have to compliment the fuel that is driving you. For instance, if your aim is to make lots of money, then it would be counter-productive to construct a small, two-seater eco-car that will only attract a few people. You should create a cult that has a broad appeal, almost indistinguishable from a normal religious institution, such that it can attract the largest number of people possible; **more minions mean more money funneled to you**. If, however, you are looking to sexually dominate and enjoy young men and/or women, you might want to consider a small cult that is focused on some bogus New Age ideology that will attract more sexually liberated people; yoga can lead to lots of physical 'hands on' exercises, if you know what I mean!

Cults can be tiny, family-sized groups with just a few dozen lost souls or they can be massive, with millions of working minions.

The scale of the cult directly reflects the desires of the Cult Leader.

If the cult is very large then it is true to say that some of the cult's energies must be given to maintaining the cult and not just satiating the Cult Leader, but this is why making a comparison with a monarchy is useful (as discussed earlier with Machiavelli's 'The Prince'). A large Kingdom needs to be supported by Knights, Lords, Barons, castle walls, armies, taxes, etc., but when it comes down to it, the King is still everything. "***It's good to be the King***". So, even when the cult, as an organization, profits from the minions, it should all still be centred around what the Cult Leader really, really wants.

For example, four years before L. Ron Hubbard started Scientology, he is reported to have said, "*If a man really wants to make a million dollars, he should start his own religion.*" Well, he did much better than that. When he died in 1986, he had hundreds of millions of dollars in his bank account. Likewise, when Japanese police raided one of the compounds owned by Shoko Asahara, they found numerous bars of gold bullion and millions of dollars in cash just lying around. It's very obvious what was motivating both Hubbard and Asahara.

Other cults seem to be started to satiate sexual desire. David Berg convinced his female followers that when they had sex with him, they were really having sex with God. Seriously! People will believe anything, won't they?

Anton Szandor LaVey convinced his 'First Church of Satan' minions that sex was an integral path to releasing Satan's energy – as long as it was the men who were being satisfied. Osho is an example of a mixed desire for wealth and sex – combining consumerism with tantrism. There's a reason why millions knew him as the 'Rolls Royce Sex Guru'!

Part 2: The Doomsday Device

This is a key component of a cult – the engine of your vehicle. Without it, you would go nowhere. **It is the fear that the device induces that makes the Indoctrination work**. Doomsday scenarios and cults have gone hand in hand from the beginning; many of the first cults to appear in history books, like the Greek Eleusinian cult, specialized in escaping the 'End of Days'.

All cults exploit the incredible ability that humans have for understanding their own mortality. This also extends into a collective recognition of how finite things are, formally known as **Endism**. This can be a literal 'end of the world', whether it is brought about through a judgement by a higher power, or by a natural process like meteors, or by human actions such as nuclear wars. It can also be framed as a personal disaster in the form of death without achieving the individual's full potential, particularly involving suicide.

No matter what form it takes, it must be seen in absolute terms. Saying, "*Things are going to get a bit bad for you.*" won't be enough of a threat to scare people into submission. Likewise, just saying, "*Hey, if you join my group, you're gonna get a bit happier and, over time, things will get better for most of us!*", is not going to cut it as an attraction either, even though, in reality, **it is the most achievable and productive goal for humans**. No. It has to be an absolute disaster, destroying everything the minions know.

The essential element of this part, however, is that you MUST offer salvation within your mythology as a way of AVOIDING a terrible catastrophe. **A person who JUST threatens catastrophe will be regarded as an annoying lunatic, but a person who threatens the same catastrophe BUT ALSO promises salvation will be regarded as a divine prophet.**

Charles Manson told his followers that the end was coming in the form of a race war that would consume America. He knew this because the lyrics in the Beatles song, 'Helter Skelter', told him so.

Marshall Applewhite started Heaven's Gate on the premise that the world would be ending and his minions could catch a ride to safety on an alien spacecraft by leaving their 'husks' (bodies) behind, otherwise known as a suicide pact. Jim Jones, who took his entire church to Guyana in South America, sold a Biblical end of the world doctrine that was fused with the idea of imminent nuclear holocaust – a fair enough suggestion, as this was during the Cold War and just after the Cuban Missile Crisis. Scientology doesn't operate on an end of world premise so much as the promise to self-improvement. As you go further up the hierarchy of Thetan levels, you attain super powers, such as thought control, telekinesis, and immortality. Yes. If you pay enough money to Scientology, you really can become immortal. There is no better way of avoiding Armageddon than by living forever!

It's important when 'installing' the Doomsday Device that it's not seen as something that is long into the future. There is no point in saying that the world will come to an end in five billion years, when the sun will go supernova; No one will care. You need to suggest that it will be within the minion's lifetime, or at least within the next few generations. This should be sufficient enough to scare the wits out of them and give you their money/adulation/naked bodies! **Don't worry about the fact that these threats have been going on for millennia; people don't think in a rational way like that. Fear blinds them to the bleeding obvious!**

A word of warning! The one thing that you shouldn't do is to give a specific date for Armageddon, particularly if it is within a few years of creating your cult; you're walking onto a garden rake if you do this. Early on in the Jehovah's Witnesses history, Charles Taze Russell set a firm timetable for when the end of the world would come, and he did this on three separate occasions. When the end obviously didn't happen, they took a big hit in membership, dropping after each date came and went.

Harold Camping, the radio host in America, predicted the Rapture six different times over the last 20 years of his life, and he did get lots of people to donate their money, but it also effectively ended his career. He had to end his radio show and shut up shop, because his brand was ruined. He became a laughing stock and was mocked wherever he went.

It really is best to just use phrases like 'imminent', 'impending', or 'close at hand'. **If you do succumb to media pressure and reluctantly give a date for Armageddon, there is a way around it. Don't worry. It's not the end of the world!**

Copy what the Taiwanese Cult Leader, Hon-Ming Chen, did to his 'Chen Tao' followers. He claimed that God would reveal Himself just before Armageddon… on worldwide television in 1998. When it obviously didn't happen, he didn't say that he had got the wrong date, which was Harold Camping's mistake – **A Cult Leader should never admit to getting anything wrong**.

No. He said God had actually revealed Himself... just in the form of all the Chen Tao followers, and that, because they had prayed so well, God decided to delay Judgement Day. Clever! Nevertheless, even some of his minions couldn't swallow this pile of doggy doo and they left the cult. So, it really would be better if you didn't give a date.

The one thing that you definitely shouldn't do, if you have given a date to the end of the world and you want to avoid embarrassing conversations, is the tactic that Shoko Asahara utilized. After he predicted that 1997 was the 'End of Days', he decided to avoid any possible failure for this date by 'inducing' Armageddon. He started stock piling Russian weapons and ordered his Aum Shinrikyo minions to build large chemical labs to create enough sarin gas to kill the human race.

Do NOT do this. It is wrong. It is never going to work; you'll be stopped before you succeed. Shoko Asahara spent the rest of his life in prison and was executed in 2018. Where is the profit in that?

So, the simple answer is – '*Don't give a date for Armageddon!*'

As an aspiring Cult Leader, it's your job to organize Armageddon to be a safe, productive, and profitable event.

Oh, yes. And don't horde Sarin Gas! That's a biggie!

Part 3: Structure of your Cult

The third decision regarding cult design is about the structure – the framework or chassis of your vehicle, if you will. It is the way that your cult defines a living space that interacts within the world.

Most people think that a cult is a small group of wackos, dancing naked around a camp fire in the middle of nowhere, screaming at each other about the end of the world… and in many cases, they'd be right – I'm sure the Manson Family did a lot of nude bonfire dancing in their time! But this isn't the only structure for a cult to operate in. Yes, the Compound Cult is a popular one, but you can also have a Closed-Societal Cult, and an Open-Societal Cult. The structure is strongly guided by what is fueling the Cult Leader.

A Compound Cult

A Compound Cult is easy to set up and maintain. It can be just the Cult Leader's home, as in the case of Fred Phelps and the Westboro Baptist Church, with a few more houses in the cul-de-sac for extra room, or Nelson DeCloud's Family, with a few camper vans in the driveway for extra room – and a quick getaway when the police became too nosy. It can also be a run-down ranch or campsite, like the Manson Family or the River Road Fellowship, respectively.

A Compound Cult is similar to a prison, in that it is easy to control and manipulate the 'inmates' (I will go into much greater detail about Indoctrination in Stage 3). It is also easier to keep the prying eyes of the Outside World, especially the inmates' family and loved ones, from seeing what is going on, although there is a specific downside to this; **the scale of a prison wall is in direct proportion to the scale of suspicion that it raises.** The other downside is that keeping people locked up really limits both the amount of money and new membership that they can bring in for you. If you are just starting out without large financial support, or if your aim for the cult is to have absolute control over young nubile bodies then a Compound Cult is for you, but if you want lots of money or power then you'll have to grow into something more.

A Closed-Societal Cult

This is a natural extension or bridge between the two main cult structures. Although the minions no longer live within one building or complex, they are cloistered within a bordered community, even if it may be part of a larger society. Both The Brethren and large sections of The Fundamentalist Mormons live within isolated communities that are open to the public but generally consist of cult members; Colorado City is a good example of this. The council, the police force, all the businesses are run by Mormons, and although they visit and have access to other cities for supplies and commerce, they largely keep to themselves. This brings in greater revenue and membership but it equally increases the risk of outside influence and infiltration.

An Open-Societal Cult

This is the one for money or power-hungry Cult Leaders, but it is the most difficult to achieve and maintain. Your minions will mix with horrible people from the Outside World, who have the annoying habit of empathically trying to save your minions from the ignorance and subjugation that you are enforcing on them… bastards! Control over what your minions will experience and understand becomes very difficult but the rewards are worth it. Cults like The Moonies, Jehovah's Witnesses and Scientology have millions of members, with billions in the bank. As a side note, it's worth remembering that you can set up mini-compounds (MC) within an Open-Societal structure, where you can do the tricky Indoctrination process first and then feed your minions into the open society. You can also use the MC to reinforce the process if your minions dare to have doubts about your legitimacy. You can call these MC's 'Social Retreats' or 'Training Centres'. The best example of this is Scientology and its Sea Org practice of sending members to ships or warehouses to be 'rehabilitated'.

The one feature that ALL of these structures need to possess is that the Outside World MUST be seen by your minions as poisonous, doomed and dangerous to 'mess' with. Obviously, the opposite is true, as <u>you</u> are the one who is toxic to the minions, but that's why it's good to **'Embrace Hypocrisy'!**

Part 4: Theme of your Cult

The next choice to make is to decide on a theme for your cult - a bit like the brand or make of the vehicle.

Themes are important because they are coded with subliminal, innate messaging that will attract or repel different social demographics, depending on their traits and characteristics. If you've ever played Dungeons & Dragons, then you'll know that there are different classes of characters like Sorcerer, Barbarian, Ranger or Rogue, and that each 'class' comes with its own attributes and qualities, strengths and weaknesses.

This is the same for cult themes and you must decide what kind of minion you want to attract and exploit. The main cult themes are Religious, Asian Fusion, Science Fiction and Pseudo Science.

Religious Theme

This is the BMW or Rolls Royce of the cult world – solid, dependable and familiar.

Most Cult Leaders opt for the religious theme as it comes pre-packaged with many of the elements that you will need to manage a successful cult; a convoluted and confusing mythology that can easily be twisted and perverted to satisfy your own desires, a deeply encoded set of values that are centred around worship and subservience that you can hijack and replace yourself as the Godhead, and a detailed set of commandments and decrees that you can interpret for your own ends without the ability for others to verify. It comes complete with iconography, literature, symbolism, and damnation; everything you'll need to confuse and scare people into submission. It's not surprising that this theme is known in the Cult Industry as the 'Cult-in-a-Box'.

As you might imagine, the Religious Theme typically attracts a demographic of pious, well-meaning, often fervent subjects, who can be very fearful of the world and ready to jump at any chance to be saved, without questioning the veracity of claims that are made. Perfect Cult Leader targets!

Another advantage to this theme is that it's easy to attract new recruits without raising any suspicion, as it is all part of a familiar social construct, E.g., Christianity. **People find it normal when a friend explains that they've joined a group that worships Jesus Christ. Worshipping aliens, on the other hand, not so much!** It's because of this that Religious-Themed cults can hide in plain sight, among the many traditional places of worship. There really is very little difference between them.

A word of warning! You need to know your stuff if you want to consistently confuse people. Jim Jones could and would quote, word for word, from The Bible to his Peoples Temple congregation, which allowed him to take things out of context and make it mean whatever he wanted it to. It was the same with David Koresh. If members of the Branch Davidians questioned him, he would recite from The Bible endlessly, until they were utterly confused or too tired to care. If you can't quote chapter and verse from whichever religious theme you have chosen, then you won't be able to wrap your minions around your little finger.

Asian Fusion Theme

This is the Nissan or Toyota of the cult world – comforting, sensitive, and eco-friendly.

Asian Fusion is where you incorporate elements of Buddhism, Taoism, Hinduism or Confucianism into the mix, muddying the waters even more. This is a much easier theme to work with as there is little structured scripture, and the religious concepts are vague and amorphous; easy to twist into any meaning to suit your own desires. Neither do you need to have that much knowledge on the subject. A weekend trip to a Buddhist or a Hindu retreat should be enough for you to call yourself a 'guru'. You just use lots of generic, 'inscrutable' phrases like, "*The clarity in Your sight is possible only by the opening of Your Third Eye on this path. Then, You can see the unseen.*"[4] **People will see you as 'mystical'!**

---

[4] You can make up any old rubbish but this one is taken from 'The Knowledge' by the Turkish cult *World Brotherhood Union Mevlana Supreme Foundation*.

Asian Fusion cults can hide under the auspice of any number of Front Groups (discussed later in Stage 3: Phase 1, Pg 84), such as meditation centres, yoga retreats, or spiritual sanctuaries. A growing social acceptance and popularity of Eastern beliefs have made these kinds of groups fairly innocuous to the public at large, and consequently, it shouldn't be too hard to find new recruits.

The only real downside to this theme comes from its greatest strength – its vagueness. Yes, it allows you to come out with almost any amount of verbal garbage, but many people will want specific instructions on how to behave and will find your cryptic, 'Hippy-Dippy' responses frustrating, leading to a high turnover. Mind you, if you want to get your hands on some young flesh…!

Sci-Fi Theme

This is the Maserati or Lamborghini of the cult world – Futuristic, flamboyant and brash.

Sci-Fi cults typically replace godheads with some form of alien species, usually by explaining that humans have mistaken aliens for gods, as in the case of 'Ashtar Galactic Command' or the 'Cosmic Circle of Fellowship'. These aliens have visited Earth and have changed the course of human history – or even created it. Cult Leaders will need to have had some sort of contact with aliens, by telepathy or abduction, and have been told that the aliens will return one day to 'pick up' the chosen few. The aliens need a representative on Earth to help them with this process and it just so happens that the Cult Leader has been picked for this difficult job. Honest!

Instead of salvation from Armageddon, recruits (your minions) need to be promised an eventual trip into space, joining with the aliens and travelling to a better world. Most of these cults, like Scientology, describe the human body as a temporary vessel for the true 'Being' inside. When L Ron Hubbard died in 1986, David Miscavige announced that Ron had "*discarded the body he had used in his lifetime to facilitate his existence in this Universe as it had ceased to be useful*" … in other words, 'had a heart attack'!

The Sci-fi Theme tends to attract very 'interesting' individuals who see themselves as logical, rational and guided by reason, but don't let that fool you; they are as confused and vulnerable as anyone else. Their main characteristic is that they love convoluted plots of mythology and they can wrap themselves up in it like a comfort blanket. They are obsessed with detail and tend to be very awkward in social situations, but they are very hard working and can bring in lots of money.

A word of warning! Gone are the days that you can make up an elaborate, far-fetched narrative like the Science Fiction novelist, L Ron Hubbard, did in 1953 when he created Scientology; a narrative of which that could be taken straight out of a 50's Science Fiction novel, and expect people to take you seriously! Nowadays, therefore, Scientologists have to deny that there is any science fiction within their belief system. Regardless of their denials, if you pass by any Scientology centre, you can still see imagery of its back story in the form of a volcano that is on many posters advertising *Dianetics*, the premiere book of Scientology doctrine. This hints at the deeper Sci-Fi mythology that awaits those willing to invest the time and money (lots of money!), as it was within this volcano that Xenu dumped the billions of alien souls that was later blown up, freeing them from their icy prisons, so that they could fly around the world, attaching themselves to the spirits of humans.

In Scientology, the goal is for the minions to pay lots of money (and I mean 'lots of money'!) for auditing sessions that allows them to free themselves of these invisible parasites – **always make them invisible as this will prevent anyone from proving you wrong!** This part of the mythology, however, is not revealed to the minions until they have climbed up many 'Thetan Levels' and invested lots of money in courses (did I mention 'lots of money'!), thus ensuring High Exit-Costs for those minions. (I will discuss such 'Exit-Costs' and other suppressive techniques later in Stage 4)

This doesn't mean to say that people no longer believe that we are being visited by aliens. You just need to be a bit more careful. Look at the success of authors like Erich von Däniken and David Icke. If they can make it work then anyone can!

Even though many of the principles and ideology between the Sci-Fi theme and other themes are the same, the strangeness of it makes it a hard sell. Your Front Groups and Indoctrination process need to be top-notch for this one to work. But when it works…!

Pseudo-Science Theme

This is the SAAB or DAEWOO of the cult world – Cutting edge, technical and obscure.

This is a relatively new theme and hasn't really been exploited yet to its full potential. It really pushes the aforementioned '**Dunning-Kruger Effect**' back on page 23, to the max.

Most people, contrary to their own opinion, have a pretty poor grasp of actual scientific fundamentals but, at the same time, they do understand that something like Quantum Theory is very important in providing an accurate description of the natural laws. As such, the general public tend to agree with scientific claims only when it sounds right to their view of the world, regardless of whether the claim contains any scientific rigor or not. This allows anyone with a basic grasp of scientific language to run confusing rings around the public, which is said to be the reason why an author like Deepak Chopra has done so well.

In a Pseudo-Science theme, a Cult Leader takes a kernel of scientific fact and smothers it with any rubbish he wants to make up to fit his desires. He then repeats that bit of scientific fact, over and over again, to legitimize his claims.

There are a few cults that have dabbled with it. The Unarius Academy of Science, for example, 'plays' with scientific ideas but still leans towards the Sci-Fi theme. In Japan, both the Ho No Hana Sanpogyo and the wonderfully titled Happy Science (Kôfuku-no-Kagaku) movement, borrows from scientific propositions. Even then though, they both lean towards either the Asian Fusion or Sci-Fi themes, as their Leaders received their knowledge from figures like Jesus, Buddha and Confucius… who might have been aliens!

So far, only commercial businesses have taken advantage of this, businesses like Homeopathy and Reflexology, but **I know it won't be long before Pseudo-Science produces a right bunch of cults**.

There's a huge market that exists of people who simultaneously distrust traditional science but will buy into any faux-science that fits within their opinions and fears. Get ready to perform psychologically-designed meditations that will de-toxify the soul!

A word of warning! The Pseudo-Science theme can lead to a short shelf-life if the Cult Leader makes the mistake of actually promising scientific results that can be independently tested. This is the mistake that Hogen Fukunaga made in his aforementioned Ho No Hana Sanpogyo cult in Japan. When his minions didn't get better from his 'scientifically-based' reflexology treatments, which of course they weren't going to as he had made it all up anyway, they took the printed results to an independent research centre. He was subsequently sued by many of those minions and is now in prison, owing millions of dollars. Not good!

Apart from not making the rookie mistake of writing any promises down to his minions, there are ways of avoiding the accusation of failed promises (as I will explain in the next Part), but you can see how the Pseudo-Science theme can be tricky.

Extra Note from the Author

There was a time in the 60's and 70's when there was a Political Theme, but most cults like The Democratic Worker's Party or The Tatenokai were short lived and would invariably end badly for the Cult Leaders involved[5]. It's also a theme that makes it difficult to continually control minions for any length of time, as it works within a human landscape, without an invisible higher power that can impose fear and damnation on the minions. Besides, most people have become so cynical about politics being a power for good that it would be nigh on impossible to get minions interested – even naïve students!

It is for these reasons that I have dropped the Political theme from my recommendations.

---

[5] Marlene Dixon was thrown out of her own group (bringing shame to the Cult industry!), and Yukio Mishima committed ritual suicide (seppuku) when his coup d'état failed. I'm sure you'll agree that this wasn't a good outcome for anyone.

Part 5: Motivational Mythology

The fifth decision regarding cult creation is the most important part: the design and overall look and feel of the vehicle, both inside and out – the model or type of car. It is what attracts minions to it in the first place and what incentivizes them to feel justified in joining your journey, enduring almost any hardship and shame that occurs along the way. Remember, a person won't tolerate abusive treatment if they think that it is for the sole benefit of a narcissistic individual like yourself (crazy, right?). **They need to believe that there is a genuine justification for their difficult journey, one that will bring peace and harmony to their lives (selfish sods!)** This part is often the most frustrating for aspiring Cult Leaders as they are being asked to come up with something that seems to benefit the minions – a proposition that should stick in the throat of any worthwhile '*Master in the Making*'... but have no fear! **You'll be coming up with stuff that will only appear to benefit them. In reality, it will still be about rewarding 'little old you'!**

The narratives and teachings that make their journey appear to be a 'Golden Ticket' to a bright new future will naturally be guided by the theme of your cult, and you are also welcome to fabricate some dogma completely from scratch, but there are some key principles and rules of design to Motivational Mythology that will help your claims to succeed.

Peerless Principle

The Peerless Principle simply states that there is ONLY one *true* 'Truth' to believe in... and it just so happens to be the Truth that YOU are peddling... honest! This is similar to Stage 1: Step 4: 'Be the One and Only' in that it triggers the **Jackpot Mentality** in humans, but it does a whole lot more. Simultaneously, it makes the minion feel lucky and grateful to have found you; he or she will become suspicious of the lies that 'false prophets' are selling in the Outside World (Nudge nudge, wink wink!); AND it makes them fearful of losing out on the only chance to find peace and harmony in their lives. They'll be both excited and scared in equal measure. **Three mental manipulations for the price of one. Bargain!**

As you'll see in Stage 3, fear is an integral part of the Indoctrination process, so if you can create something that can be both a carrot and a stick, simultaneously, it will be highly productive in controlling your minions.

An easy way to suggest that your cult is the only one to go for is by giving it a suitable name; Chen Tao means 'The True or Right Way', and Aum Shinrikyo means 'Universal or Absolute Truth'. But the simplest tactic is to repeat, over and over again, that your Truth is the only truth that is true; **repetition is a vital factor for Indoctrination**. Then let Groupthink and peer pressure do the rest.

This doesn't mean, however, that you actually have to come up with something original or different within your mythology. Quite the opposite! The LAST thing that you should do is introduce new ideas or concepts that would be unfamiliar to your minions. This was a mistake that Shoko Asahara made when he first attempted to create a cult, back in the early 80's. He tried, twice, to develop a mythology based upon wizardry and witchcraft, which would have grown well in places like California or Cornwall, but instead fell on stony ground in Japan. It was only when he went with the Buddhist legends that it was 'third time lucky' for him, as his seed found fertile soil with Aum Shinrikyo.

The lesson from this is to always appropriate the familiar. Don't create, just incorporate. Assimilate, not originate!

For example, UFO cults like Scientology and Raëlism couldn't have existed before space travel and society's desire for all things 'Out of this World' had become popular. Although there had been interest in alien life before the 1950's, it was really when rockets capable of reaching outer space were being developed during the Second World War, that space exploration and the concept of intelligent visitors from other planets became a staple for literature and film. In the 1950's, there was a glut of Sci-Fi films like - 'The Day the Earth Stood Still' (1951), 'The Thing from Another World' (1951)', and 'It Came from Outer Space' (1953); most of which were developed from stories written by Pulp Fiction authors.

Robert A. Heinlein, for example, wrote a Sci-Fi novel in 1951 called 'The Puppet Masters' about invisible aliens that attach themselves to humans in order to control them. This sounds very much like part of the Scientology mythology that Hubbard, a Pulp Fiction writer himself, developed a few years later. Now, I am not saying that Hubbard stole the idea from this novel… but if he had, he would have done the right thing – Don't create, incorporate!

You must *tell* your minions that what you have is unique but, in reality, you must always appropriate the familiar.

Righteous Principle

Humans seem hardwired to thrive on perceived associations with righteous choices, so much so that they will continue with a plan of action or a way of life, even when it has a negative effect on them. Why is this, you may ask?

As a species, in order to maintain the very beneficial effects of a supportive, social system, we have developed the notion of fairness and morality. This is at odds with the amoral universe of Cause and Effect, and therefore there is often a disparity between what we want to happen to us in the world and what actually happens to us; **a gap between hope and reality**.

This disparity or gap is one of the major sources of people's frustrations and insecurities in their lives; otherwise known as the Why Me Disorder (WMD)[6]. To bridge this gap, many techniques have been developed, such as Cognitive Behavioral Therapy, that can help the individual to change their expectations and actions. Over time, they cultivate a level of acceptance that makes them see the bad times as part of life, leading to a focus on the good times. Obviously, the last thing you should do as a Cult Leader is actually help your minions to make these changes! This would increase their levels of contentment and confidence, making it very difficult to manipulate and subjugate them. A disaster for any Cult Leader!

---

[6] The Germans, who are steeped in psychoanalysis, know WMD as Weltschmerz.

What you need to do is present a false hope to your minions within your mythology which states that there IS a way of finding perfection and absolute happiness in THIS world, and that being associated with YOUR virtuous cause is the ONLY way to succeed.

As this imperfect world continues to let them down, their levels of frustration, confusion and insecurities will go up, establishing the perfect conditions for controlling the minion.

Your mythology should pretend to bridge this gap of disparity by providing a 'designed' justification for the discrepancy, making them fool themselves into thinking that there is 'a reason for it all'. Don't worry! You don't actually have to provide the perfect solution, as we both know there is no such thing. You just need an appealing narrative that your minions can buy into.

In other words, you must give your minions a hook to hang their mental shroud of delusion onto.

Does this sound familiar? Yes, it is our old friend **Cognitive Dissonance** again, as discussed back in Stage 1: Step 3, Page 28. This time, instead of just utilizing this human trait, you need to ramp it up by providing an external excuse for their internal deceit. There are a couple of handy hooks that can help you.

Your mythology could contain the notion that there is suffering in the world because humans are being tested to see if they are worthy of being the 'chosen'. This is a useful hook as it allows you to really pile on the cruelty, whilst making your minions see the suffering as a good thing, providing the proof of their worthiness. In fact, the journey is made all the more special BECAUSE of the deprivation and hardship. The notion that an easy life is not worth living is common place. Take this quote from President Theodore Roosevelt – "*Nothing in the world is worth having or worth doing unless it means effort, pain, difficulty...*", or this from the Buddha – "*I'm not telling you it's going to be easy. I'm telling you it's going to be worth it*". This is perfect fodder for minions to feed on.

You could actually say that it is your duty to cause suffering for your minions, as they will benefit more from the abusive, painful journey that you have created... you could say that!

The other hook that increases **Cognitive Dissonance** is the idea that the minions themselves are the reason for the discrepancy between what should happen and what does happen; that things would be perfect if only the minions could always get things right. This one is a doozie and I like to call it **'The Circle of Servitude'**! It goes like this – Life is not what it should be, therefore your minions feel scared and insecure. You promise them a path to enlightenment, but because life is not what it should be, they fail to succeed on that path. You blame them for the failure, which increases their fear and self-doubt. You promise them a path to enlightenment, but because life is not what it should be, yes, you've guessed it, they fail again. Boom! You've got them going around in circles, chasing their tails.

If you are doubtful about the success of this process then take a look at another billion-dollar business that employs this tactic – The Diet Industry! For decades, research has proven that diets fail – particularly over the long term – AND that they actually work AGAINST the physiological and neurological mechanisms of the human body. Diets have a failure rate of over 80% (Traci Mann, UCLA). The Diet Industry, however, continually shifts the blame for this failure onto the dieters, and repeatedly claim that a perfect body/shape/weight is achievable, ONLY if their particular diet is maintained, even though there is no such thing as a perfect... anything! The fact is that the Diet Industry NEEDS dieters to fail or else they would go out of business. It is the same with cults.

You can increase the effectiveness of this process by introducing difficult or nigh-on impossible expectations within the mythology. Use the narrative to suggest that denying basic human emotions like jealousy, anger or lust is beneficial, or that it is vital to completely surrender to a higher power at the expense of all else, including family. These kinds of challenges, that go against the human psyche, will have them doomed for failure.

There are also a couple of simple rules that you should consider for the success of your mythology.

The Fantastic Rule

Whatever you make up, don't be afraid to put a few crazy, extraordinary stories into the mix. It may seem like a good idea to keep things reasonable and believable, but you'll be giving humans too much credit AND missing out on a trick. Claims like receiving gifts from Angels (Joseph Smith: Mormonism), aliens using your eyes as remote cameras (Claude Vorilhon: Raëlism), or gaining super powers like telepathy and telekinesis (L Ron Hubbard: Scientology), will all be accepted by your minions. **Don't worry, people will believe almost anything if you tell it with confidence and certainty (Remember Stage 1: Step 2: Always be Certain).** It will also have two beneficial effects on them… benefits for you, that is. Firstly, it will force your minions to dig deeper into their irrational thought processes – aiding you with the molding of them (Discussed later in Stage 3). Secondly, it will add to the High Exit-Costs for your minions (Discussed later in Stage 4), as they will have to admit to their loved ones that they actually believed in your made-up garbage. This is difficult to do at the best of times, but when someone has low self-esteem, it becomes nearly impossible; think of a battered wife who has continually defended her abusive husband from the accusations by her family, trying to admit that she was wrong. That's the kind of emotional control that you should be aiming for!

The Nothing-In-Between Rule

Always give the morality in your stories a Binary Landscape of 'All or Nothing'; leaving no room for ambiguity. This **Forced Dichotomy** of Good v Evil, Light v Dark, Weak v Strong, Truth v Lie, and Friend v Enemy will force your minions into accepting your biased view of the world – giving them no choice at all – "*Are you with me or against me?*", "*Do you want to be weak or strong?*" This will blind them to the complex, graded nature of life, preventing them from using a balanced, critical understanding of their choices. This process will help you to mold them into what you want them to be… but more about that soon.

Part 6: Funding your Cult

The final question to answer in building your vehicle is one of finance; what kind of a car can you afford? There's no point in designing a Lamborghini when you can only afford a tiny Skoda; we can't all be as lucky as Sun Myung Moon was, when he struck gold with one of his first converts to his Unification Church being a Billionaire Industrialist. It meant that Rev. Moon could not just build a Lamborghini, he bought some for his children. Lucky Dog!

Like any professional business, a cult takes upfront financial investment. You might have a compound to build, leaflets and posters to print in order to disseminate your propaganda… I mean, your words of wisdom, and even if you are housing a bunch of minions within your own home, you will still need to feed them, (although the costs can be minimized by just giving them rice and water - "*Sacrifice is good, blah blah blah*"!)

So, where to start? Well, there is both good news and bad news.

First, the bad news.

Unfortunately, there is a good deal of prejudice within the banking world towards the Cult Industry. You can't exactly go into your local bank and get a small business loan for a cult start-up. This is extremely shortsighted of them, given that many cults become spectacularly wealthy, and it's not as if most banks have any ethics on screwing customers over for whatever they can get out of them; you'd think an abusive cult would be right up their alley but, sadly, there it is.

The good news is though, that there are multiple revenue sources for a Cult Leader to exploit, and I've listed most of them for you.

Monetize Your Minions

I know it seems obvious but your minions are your livelihood and you need to treat them as such. **Never forget the Golden Rule:**

A MINION IS THE GIFT THAT KEEPS ON GIVING!

Minions can be monetized in a number of ways, dependent upon the structure of the cult that you have chosen.

A Compound or Closed-Societal structure limits the amount of money that a minion can earn, so go for their possessions and savings - they won't need them in the prison that you've created. To make them happy for you to do this, sell them the idea that they should 'free' themselves of the trappings of worldly possessions, with phrases like – "*You don't own your possessions, your possessions own you!*". Tell them that money is the root of all evil, and then sell their stuff on eBay to get as much money for yourself as possible! You can also make your minions borrow from friends and family as a form of investment in what they are doing. This will be short-lived for each minion, as their loved ones will soon wise up, and you'll also be getting your minions to break ties with them anyway (see 'Disconnection' in Stage 4: Level 1, page 120), but you might as well use the opportunity whilst it is there.

The only way to keep money coming in on a regular basis with a Compound Cult is to use your minions as slave labour. This is done in two ways. You can use them as slave labour for the cult itself, building and maintaining the compound, with extensions and extras when and where necessary – you will never need to hire a cleaner, a cook, or a plumber when you have a minion at your feet! This really keeps the running costs for your cult to a minimum.

You can also use their labour outside of the cult, although you will need to minimize their interaction with other people to do this. Charles Manson made members of his Family give horseback riding tours on the land around their Spahn Ranch in California to City Slickers who wanted to 'get back to nature' for an afternoon. Stewart Traill of The Church of Bible Understanding used his minions within his cleaning company, both as admin and front-line workers. He was able to undercut any competitor because his running costs where nearly zero. Marshall Applewhite had a few of his Heaven's Gate minions work for his 'Higher Source' web-design business. Most of the interactions with their clients were done over the phone.

Many of your minions won't have advanced employment skills but all of them could mow a lawn, paint a wall or clean a room. This makes setting up a small local business as easy as printing up flyers and advertising on Craig's List. No paychecks to sort out, no HR hassles or tax deductions. Oh, and don't keep any work records so that your minions will have nothing to show for their time in your cult, just in case they try to leave (High Exist-Costs).

In an Open-Societal cult, minions who live in a 'normal way' will sadly have bills to pay and will need to afford a certain level of lifestyle, therefore, expecting them to give ALL their money to you is unrealistic, about 20% of their wages should be alright... especially if they are earning millions within businesses like the film industry; Tom Cruise must be seen as a Golden Goose to Scientology! This doesn't mean, however, that you can't screw them for even more money. You can create courses and lectures that they have to go on, set up donation drives that they have to contribute to, and then there's all the merchandise that they have to pay for; all of which is to help them find independence and a life free from cruelty and corruption... don't ya just love the irony! Along with getting them to leave everything in their will to you, you can really see how minions in an Open-Societal cult are worth their weight in gold.

Literature and Merchandise

Most cults, from Hare Krishna to Jehovah's Witness, Family of God to Scientology, have a wide variety of literature, DVD's and knick-knacks which are produced from within the cult. Some of this merchandise is distributed for free as part of the recruitment process to draw people in – 'something for nothing', but most of it will be available for purchase, both by the unsuspecting public and by the minions themselves. It is easy nowadays to create a library of literature from your 'teachings' by getting your minions to write down everything you've said, cutting and pasting as you go.

Make sure that you do many different versions of what you say so that you can avoid any accusation of contradiction by explaining that "*different versions apply to different people*". On that note, it's a good idea to do a 'self-help' version of your books, feeding off of the Self-help Industry that rakes in over 10 billion dollars every year. You might as well get a piece of that action!

It's also a good idea to get your minions to make trinkets, like bracelets and necklaces, to hand to each other and polite outsiders. It won't cost much, it seems harmless, but it keeps them busy... busy, busy, busy.

The most important aspect of the merchandise is that you sell it to your captive market, your minions. They will need to buy EVERY version of your books, ALL the DVD's and CD's, and every trinket made to complete their collection. They must buy every single item to prove that they have succeeded in being free from possessions!

Charitable Donations

You should always pretend that your cult is doing charitable work in the world, and therefore need donations from members and non-members alike to continue the good fight; you might even get tax-exemptions from the government. Don't worry if this charitable work includes building a pool in your own backyard; most people don't investigate the organizations that they give money to. This is also a good reason why you should have lots of children in your cult, as they are brilliant at emotionally blackmailing people into parting with their money, but more about that in Stage 5: Lesson 4: Influential Innocence, page 14**6**.

Front Groups

We will explore Front Groups in greater detail in the next stage but, for now, it's worth saying that the best-structured Front Groups don't just provide one-off courses or individual workshops, rather than a series of them, all increasing in cost. This allows people, whether they become minions or not, to give an eye-watering amount of money to you. A quick Google search for 'motivational seminars' or 'spiritual retreats' will prove to you how these sorts of fatuous, inane self-improvement courses are a booming industry, with millions of people ready to pay large sums of money to excrete non-existent toxins out of their skin at an 'authentic' Sweat Lodge in Arizona! "*A fool and his money are soon parted*"!

Checklist for Stage 2

So, if you have done what I told you to do, and carefully followed my fool-proof **6**-Part template, you should be the proud owner of a well-constructed, lean, mean driving machine.

You will have been honest with yourself about what you really, really want, and have been pragmatic about how you are going to go about it. You will have spent a bit of time thinking about the kind of minion you want to attract, and what kind of Cult Theme that will draw those minions towards you, like a moth to a flame.

You will have spent some time on developing your unique, unparalleled mumbo-jumbo that all your minions will be familiar with and get excited by – don't forget that it should also scare the crap out of them as well!

Finally, you will have prepared the various funding streams for maintaining your cult, so that you have a long and productive journey ahead of you.

In other words, you should be firmly in the driving seat of a solid, seductive vehicle for your desires.

Are you ready to take people for a ride? Do you have what it takes to drive such a lethal weapon as this car? Let's find out…

End of Stage 2 Quiz

Answer the questions below and see how you have scored.

Question 1) Why is it important to be honest about what you want from your cult?

A) I don't want anything from my cult. I'm a giver!

B) I don't run a cult. I'm head of a peaceful organization that provides positive guidance. Don't you dare say otherwise!

C) It is counter-productive to invest in something that won't provide you with a genuine satisfaction.

Question 2) Which Cult Theme promotes sexual freedom?

A) The 'Asian Fusion' Theme, as yoga and tantric exercises provide plenty of 'hands on' opportunities.

B) It doesn't matter. I'm free to have sex with anyone I want. I am King of the Castle.

C) It doesn't matter. Sexual abuse is wrong.

Question 3) When would a Cult Leader transition the structure of his cult from Open-Societal to Compound?

A) When he wants to avoid deeper scrutiny by the Outside World.

B) When he wants to heighten his control over all his minions.

C) When his paranoia has got the better of him.

Question 4) Who would believe in bizarre mythology that was clearly imaginary?

A) Someone who is desperate for meaning in their lives.

B) Imaginary? Every word I say is the absolute truth!

C) A person who is not used to applying Critical Thinking.

Question 5) When would you give a date for Armageddon?

A) Never. I would be proved wrong.

B) Never… unless I had enough weaponry to induce it!

C) Never. It's a fabricated concept that can lead to tragedy.

Question 6) What is the main consideration when it comes to funding your cult?

A) How to find as many revenue streams as possible.

B) How to screw your minions out of every penny, even after they are dead!

C) How to share the rewards with everyone in the group, providing a sense of self-worth for each individual.

How did you do?

Mostly A's – You are firing on all cylinders. Go on to Stage 3.

Mostly B's – You've created a sporty little number but you need to check the torque on the engine. Read Part 2 again.

Mostly C's – You've built a vehicle for kindness and humanity… and you should be ashamed of yourself; it won't leave the garage. Change your ways and start seeing people as objects… or else!

Stage Three:
Molding Your Minions

Let's review your progress so far -

You have transformed yourself into, what could be seen as, a charismatic Cult Leader, and you have created a motivational vehicle for your desires. Great!

Notice anything missing? How about the minions?

Without the minions, you don't actually have a cult. Without the minions, you are just standing alone in an empty space, saying meaningless things to thin air. And if that's what you want to do… you should become a politician!

No! Now that you have created a product for people to buy into, you can't just sit back and wait for the 'till to ring'; cults don't sell themselves, you know?... Not in the early stages of them anyway. And there is no point in shouting from the rooftops – "*I've got a cult that I want to abuse people with so that I can live a life of luxury and pleasure, at the expense of those abused people!*" Strangely enough, it won't work. Don't get me wrong, there are many people who are tired of making decisions for themselves and secretly want to be led and controlled, but even they won't openly accept it. You'll have to fool them into becoming your servants. You can do this by guiding them through the '**6** Phases of Metamorphosis', transforming them from thoughtful, independent individuals into meek and malleable minions.

Before we get into those **6** phases, I want to spend a few moments on a couple of principles that are fundamental to this whole Stage; **Gradualism** and **Indoctrination**.

Gradualism

More accurately known as **Creeping Normality, t**his is the principle that a major change in a person's life, particularly one that is objectionable or harmful, can be easily accepted if it is done through small and often unnoticeable, incremental steps. Obviously, the phrase '*Death by a Thousand Cuts*' springs to mind, but the best analogy I can give is that of the home of a Hoarder.

You may know someone who has a problem with hoarding or you might have seen TV programs about such people, but we can all imagine that kind of house that has piles and piles of rubbish in every room, clearly inhibiting and harming the Hoarders life, even though, they themselves can't see it. The point is that it didn't start out like that. It might have started with just a bit of mess or a single collection of items that the Hoarder was interested in, and, as they got used to that new environment and it became the norm, the next bit of mess or new collection also wouldn't seem strange to the Hoarder… then the next slight change, and the next slight change, until eventually, the Hoarder is living in a squalid dump. People from the outside can't understand why or how the Hoarder can live like this but, to the Hoarder, it is perfectly normal.

This is EXACTLY the same dynamic for a minion in a cult.

Family and friends can scream at their loved one until their throats are raw, for being in such an abusive situation - that is until you've banned your minion from seeing them (see **Disconnection** on page 120 for more details), but the screams will fall onto deaf ears because the minion will have been subjected to your incremental changes, making them view their subjugation as 'the norm' – to the point that they actually view the Outside World as the crazy place!

Indoctrination

The word 'Indoctrination' is regularly banded about by politicians, the media, and people who attend the launch of a new Apple product, but it is rarely explained properly. Given that Indoctrination is so vital for a Cult Leader, it's worth taking our time to get a clear understanding of what it is and how it works.

It originally meant a form of education through continual instruction, like learning the times tables through repetition, but the negative form of the word involves **a process of learning that demands, usually through a threat of punishment, a lack of critical thinking and examination** – a "*do as you're told and just accept what I say*" form of education. You know, the kind of education from the 1950's… or in China today!

If your minions are learning through detailed enquiry and open exploration… then you are doing it wrong. They should accept, without question or understanding, the claims and lessons that you are giving. The moment someone asks analytical, critical questions about what you are saying, you know the Indoctrination has failed.

That is the theory, but the big question is '*How does a Cult Leader actually implement Indoctrination?*' There are **6** factors that need to be in place for Indoctrination to work.

1) The education must come from an Authoritarian Instructor; no friendly, sympathetic teachers allowed here. This should already be the case if you have been successful at becoming a Cult Leader (Stage 1).

2) The content of the 'education' should play to their fears and weaknesses; "*Do you want the world to be destroyed? Are you a man or a mouse?*" This should be covered by the Motivational Mythology that you have created in Stage 2 (Page **65**).

3) Fear of failure or punishment must be ever-present in the minds of the minions; "*Do you want to die a failure?*" **Fear is an integral part of Indoctrination.**

4) Critical Thinking and Individual Independence must be inhibited and eventually nullified. We will cover this later in Phase 4 and 5, respectively.

5) An environment of Peer Pressure must pile on the need to conform and accept what is being told to the minion.

6) **Repetition must be practiced at all times.**

This last factor is so important that it needs to be repeated.

Repetition must be practiced at all times.

This last factor is so important that it needs to be repeated.

Repetition must be practiced at all times.

Why is repetition so useful when it comes to indoctrinating someone into a particular view or way of life?

Repetition is one of the mechanisms that strengthen the connections (axons) between the neurons within the brain, thus allowing difficult tasks to become automated – think about changing gears when driving a car. At first it takes focus to change the gears, using lots of neural energy, but after much repeated practice, it becomes instinctual, meaning less energy. The neuro-psychologist, Donald Webb, aptly described this process when he said – "*Neurons that fire together, wire together.*" The stronger those neurons are wired together, the more difficult it is to re-wire them. **The very neurological processes of the brain mean that humans are hard-wired to value repetition over reason. This allows false or flawed concepts to triumph over factually accurate ones, if repeated enough.** Take advantage of this trait by using repetition to validate your claims to 'The Truth'… whatever truth you have just made up!

Through practice, you will see how Indoctrination works and it's important to understand that all of this is a gentle, gradual process of incremental Phases of control that will constantly ebb and flow, as the minion sometimes resists the change and other times accepts it hook, line and sinker. Think of it in terms of fishing. Sometimes you'll want to pull back on the fishing rod to hold onto the fish, but then let the reel go for a while so that the fish tires itself out.

It's also important to note that your minions will need to be exposed to a regular regime of maintenance techniques… but that's for Stage 4! For now, let's get molding your minions…

As we are talking of 'gentle, gradual processes', we will start with an easy one. Phase 1 of the transformation…

Phase 1: Fishing with Front Groups

Before you can mold anyone into a minion, you have to gain access to them first. Approaching people in the street or at their front door is a very 'hit-and-miss' affair… and can lead to arrests, so you'll need a more ordered and less confrontational way of luring people in. This is why **Front Groups** are vital. They are organizational platforms, that offer you a useful and seemingly harmless access point to a potential minion, as well as earning income for your cult. They can take many forms, such as self-improvement workshops, small businesses, meditation retreats, yoga classes, or good old-fashioned therapy programs. All of them appear to be there to help the initiated, but are really hiding the true cult that is waiting in the shadows to use and abuse the new recruit.

In other words, the Front Group is the smile of a crocodile.

Who should you fish for? It is a general misconception that Cult Leaders should only target stupid, gullible losers to be minions. This is wrong because, although it will be easy to mold them, you will just be left with stupid loser minions, who will continually make mistakes and ruin your cult in the long run. You will be missing out on a rich stream of targets if you only take the easy option. The fact is that anybody has the potential for becoming a minion. This is so important that it is worth repeating –

Anybody has the potential for becoming a minion.

Whether they are young or old, rich or poor, highly intelligent or state educated; it doesn't matter. The key factor to look out for is whether they are vulnerable at the point of contact or '*when the line is cast*', to continue with the analogy. These people are known as Temporarily Vulnerable Targets (TVT's). Perhaps someone has just gone through a really messy break-up, or even better, has had a life-long partner die on them! Perhaps someone has made a radical career change or have up-rooted and moved to a new area and are looking to make a fresh start. ANY kind of situation that makes a person question where he or she is going in their lives can make for a good TVT.

Obviously, the logical thing for humans to do in these hazardous conditions would be to pay extra caution to the world around them, taking their time before making any crucial decisions, but luckily for us, most people aren't logical (regardless of how rational they think they are!), and it is common for humans to be openly vulnerable at these times. Foolish but, hey… better for us, right?

This doesn't mean that you shouldn't be casting towards people who have low self-esteem or high levels of gullibility, like drug addicts or conspiracy theorists, but you should never ignore the people who would normally laugh at your made-up crap, as they could, at a time of weakness, be reeled in by your false promises.[7]

A word of caution. The sort of person you must avoid is a skeptic, who arrogantly asks annoying questions like – "*Do you have verifiable evidence for what you are saying?*" or "*Can you provide any citations for your claims?*"! They will create ripples in the water, disturbing the other fish that you are trying to catch. Just accuse them of trying to sabotage other people's happiness and get rid of them as quickly as possible.

One of the first tactics that I'll be talking about later in this Stage is to make your minions feel inadequate and unworthy. **Thus, it only makes sense to target people who already feel insecure. Front Groups are perfect for this**. They are self-selecting because most people are going to seminars, workshops or retreats to improve themselves anyway. A neat trick is to set up a Front Group near a fast-food place AND a fitness centre. It won't be long before you'll see someone slumped over a table in the restaurant, with a gym bag at their feet, tucking into a double-cheeseburger. It's a safe bet that they'll be at a moment of weakness and you could mention that you are about to go into this amazing seminar about self-control. Boom! Hook, line and sinker!

---

[7] David Berg, who created Family of Love, would send his female minions out to entice men back to the cult with the promise of sex. He called it 'Flirty Fishing' and it's a good analogy for how Front Groups operate.

Like any good fisherman, your Front Group should change the bait to match the fish that you are trying to catch. For example, Osho adapted his meditation seminars in the 1970's to incorporate the then-new American psychological exercises of aggressive ego-breaking, as he was getting many wealthy disillusioned Americans travelling to India to 'discard' their corrupt lives. David Berg created a Front Group in California to fish the rich stream of highly intelligent student drop-outs who were trying to 'fight the system'. He baited them with free love and no rules… except for the strict rules that he had made up for them. **Raëlism is one of the few cults that doesn't have a Front Group. It just baits people with sex orgies… which actually works remarkably well!**

Many religious-themed cults will present a 'watered-down' friendly version of themselves to the public, usually in the form of 'Discovery Groups' or 'Inclusive Faith Centres'. They present an image of a warm and supportive community… without mentioning the Disconnection with non-members, strict draconian regulations, and, in the case of the Jehovah's Witnesses, the inability to celebrate birthdays or receive a formal education.

By far, however, the cult that most effectively utilizes Front Groups is Scientology. To most of the world, Scientology is simply a series of 'Orgs', whereby members of the public can visit and pay to go on courses that purport to help them with relationships and other life skills, completely oblivious to the dark, abusive cult that lies deep within the organization.

Additionally, Scientology operates The Hubbard Management System, which runs seminars at corporate centres around the globe, and has an entire series of expensive courses that can be taken by external company employees. Scientology also runs Narconon, a global drug rehabilitation program that purports to have a 90% success rate... although they have cleverly never provided independent citation for that number! Narconon even has had government contracts around the world to provide its services to drug courts and probation departments, though recently a number of attendance deaths have caused these contracts to be terminated.

But it doesn't stop there. Oh, no! Criminon (apparently, just adding the suffix 'non' to any word makes it sound official!), a program meant to lower the reoffending rate amongst criminals, is yet another arm of Scientology. And then there are the Scientology education programs, detoxification centres and personality workshops.

Can you guess what factor runs through all of these paid programs? Beyond providing a profitable income for the cult, and a public face of legitimacy, each of these Front Groups self-selects lost and damaged individuals who are desperate and vulnerable. The Front Groups provide a supposed safe and supportive environment for people to slowly, step by step, be introduced to the tenets and beliefs of Scientology. Then, and only then, are people chosen to 'Cross the Bridge' and get drawn into the actual cult itself; but more about that later. Scientology really does have it sewn up, and I don't expect you to match them straight off. It's just something to aim for in the long run.

For now, what's important is to create a friendly, supportive and comforting system that can draw people in.

Talking of 'friendly, supportive and comforting'…

Phase 2: Love Bombing

So, you should now have a room full of disillusioned teenagers, depressed housewives, or spiritually lost people with low self-esteem, eager to change their lives.

How are they managed?

First, make sure the room is mixed with new and older, more experienced, committed minions of your cult – you never want a large group of new recruits on their own; older recruits should always outnumber the new recruits. These experienced minions will then proceed to **Love Bomb** the new recruits, whereby they smile at them all the time, hug and compliment them, and make them feel valued, loved and welcomed.

Apparently, humans like this sort of crap!

Don't challenge the new recruits directly on anything that they say, encouraging a need for them to 'keep an open mind'... laying the ground work for you to close their minds tight shut later. Everybody should express a deep connection with each other and how much they enjoy a place where they can be themselves without fear of judgement - you gotta keep '**Embracing Hypocrisy**'. Make the new recruits want to come back for a second session... and a third. Make them feel like they are part of the group, that maybe they've found some new friends or even a potential 'family'. **Love Bombing works remarkably well at lowering a person's defenses**.

Increasingly though, as the sessions continue, you make this 'love' conditional; nothing serious at first, just very subtle changes. Using the psychology of group dynamics (**Groupthink**), if a new recruit questions or doubts the claims that are being made, your more experienced minions will begin to withhold their affection, dropping the smile, creating awkward silences, looking at each other uneasily. Once the new recruit expresses sentiments that are in line with those being taught, the affection immediately returns.

This is formally known as **Operant Conditioning** and was popularized in the 1930's by Professor B F Skinner.

The process reinforces the idea that, '**Conformity – Good, Independent Thinking – Bad**'. It's not dissimilar to training a dog: A Good dog gets treats – A Bad dog gets left out in the cold.

This kind of group coercion or **Herd Mentality** really works; people are far more malleable than they want to believe. Many studies have proven this to be true – one of the most famous being the **Asch Conformity Experiment**.

The Asch Paradigm

In 1951, a psychologist called Solomon Asch invited students from a Pennsylvanian university to carry out a task that was supposedly looking at perception skills. A group of 'students' were brought into a room and given two cards. On the first card was a single straight line (marked x) and the other card had three straight lines of varying lengths on it, one of which matched the length of the line on the first card.

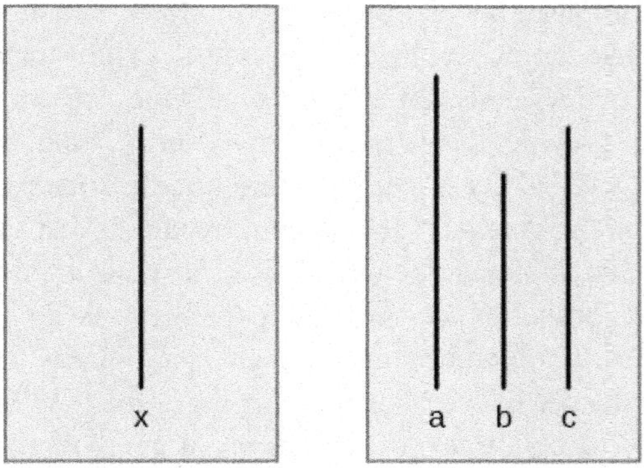

Each volunteer was then asked to say out loud – and it's very important for them to say it out loud, which line they thought matched the 'x' line (a, b, or c). A simple task, yes?

C, right?

In reality, the test was looking at group coercion and there was only one genuine 'test subject' in each group – the other 'students' being in on the experiment (very much like a Front Group of a cult), and they were following their instructions to give the wrong answer each time (answering B, for example). These 'plants' would answer incorrectly, even though it was obvious which line was the same, but by the time it got to the genuine test subject, 75% of them would fit in and give the wrong answer as well, rather than stand out from the crowd by giving the right answer… **75%**!

This may seem like a superficial and simplistic test, but don't forget that this was done as a stand-alone experiment with a group of strangers, in a cold, clinical environment. Imagine the kinds of pressures that could be created if your minions were to be placed in a large, family-style environment, over a period of months or even years. It is the **Herd Mentality** that allows an individual to rid themselves of their own values, and replace them with the cult's values. **Over time, you'd be amazed at how much you can change the social and ethical landscape of your minions. Today, it is the measure of a straight line. Tomorrow, it could be the measure of a person's worth.**

A good example of how this dynamic is utilized is found within the Alpha Course, organized by Nicky Gumbel. The Alpha Course is a series of free sessions that "*explores life, faith and meaning*", and is said to provide "*an opportunity to hear from others and contribute your own perspective in an honest, friendly and open environment.*" What participants don't realize is that many of the seasoned church members 'join in' with the new initiates. It's not uncommon for there to be only a couple of genuine new recruits in groups of 8-10 individuals, of which everyone else will be a long-standing member of the church. This gives the new initiates the appearance of being part of a large swell of exploration, which makes it easier for them to form attachments with their co-voyagers on an epic adventure of discovery.

At these sessions, the participants are really made to feel welcome with smiling, friendly faces, hugs and laughter, music, free food, and the ready opportunity to have an instantly accessible network of new friends – provided, of course, that they conform.

When the inevitable questions about faith and God arise – the very subjects that the Alpha Course advertise as being carried out in a 'friendly and open environment', and doubts are expressed over the subject-matter, the church members withhold the affection and start separating the 'awkward' people away from the 'potential' ones, from session to session. Eventually, as the weeks go by, the 'potentials' uncannily end up in one group, and the awkward people are isolated from the rest with the hope that they just leave.

If you want to see how this dynamic works, sign up to an Alpha Course yourself. They are usually free and can be found in most cities. Now that you know how they work, watch in awe at how people are manipulated. It's fantastic!

Love Bombing also triggers a common fallacy called the **Halo Effect**, whereby a single experience or characteristic of a person or group (like a lovely evening of friendship, music and smiles) will be then forever attributed to that person or group as a whole (always seeing the group and leader as friendly and lovely, regardless of how abusive and harmful they become). It will help to immunize the minions from seeing the reality of how bad you and your cult will be to them… and others.

Love Bombing is a friendly, non-threatening way of starting the process of change, and few people will suspect anything. The downside to it is that the control that it provides is fairly limited; a tasty carrot can only do so much… we need to introduce some sticks. But before we start smacking our minions with sticks… metaphorically speaking, of course… (Nudge, nudge, wink, wink!) we need to build a solid foundation to prepare them for the changes ahead. We need to give them even more of a reason to go through the tough journey that awaits them.

The next Phase is centred around an idea that they will already be familiar with, but now, we need to take it up a notch...

Phase 3: Demonize the Outside World

If you've been following my advice, you should already have developed the notion that the world is '*going to hell in a handcart*', and that YOUR path is the ONLY direction to take; only a balanced individual, who actually wants to help people to find happiness, would state that there are multiple ways of finding success in life... but where is the profit in that? So, it is a no-brainer to encourage the idea that your group is the only way forward – remembering not to call it a cult, as people have a biased view that cults are bad.

But this Phase is far more important than that. It has **6** beneficial qualities that makes it essential for you to 'ramp it up to the max'.

Quality 1: Playing to the Gallery

As discussed, the recruits will have joined the Front Group to improve their lives, or to avoid being seen as a failure by their family, or to find some kind of a semblance of meaning in their pitiful excuse of an existence. So, listing what is wrong with the world and promising to save them will be '*succor to an infant*', or as we like to say in the industry – "**Use succor to create a sucker!**"

It plays to their anxieties and fears, which, as mentioned, is a vital factor for Indoctrination. The recruit must be supported in their suspicions about the flawed world around them, and they must be encouraged to find a better one within the cult. This way, they will feel lucky to have found you... which leads to...

Quality 2: A Carrot-shaped Stick

As discussed in Stage 2: Part 5: Motivational Mythology on page **65**, your teachings should be seen as a 'Golden Ticket' to a journey of discovery that will lead your recruits to a bright new future. This will trigger the **Jackpot Mentality** in them and they should be excited to be a part of it. To begin with, encourage this excitement. But then, progressively, turn the carrot into a stick by threatening the recruits with losing out on this journey if they don't play their part in the group, in other words, conform. By the end, they should see leaving the group as a fatal move... literally, and see anyone outside of the group as corrupt and doomed... which leads to...

Quality 3: A Vaccine from Infection

Depending on the structure of your cult, seeing the Outside World as evil and dangerous can help with the separation and distancing of your minions from nosy, interfering family, friends and anyone who has a critical thought process. Obviously, a Compound Cult won't need this quality so much, but it most definitely will be needed with Closed or Open-Societal Cults. Your minions will often come into contact with dangerous influences, sometimes without any supervision, so they must have an ever-present suspicion and even aversion to people from the Outside World. They MUST see those people as evil and damned; not an easy thing to do when humans are so… human…

Quality 4: Dehumanize the Enemy

Humans are a social species and therefore instinctively identify with other humans. This phenomenon is commonly seen at times of war. It has been repeatedly observed that most soldiers would rather shoot into the air, or not even pull the trigger, rather than kill another human being. This does not make for a successful soldier. So, the main technique to overcome this 'flaw' is to Dehumanize the Enemy, sometimes referred to as '**Atrocity Propaganda**'. The propaganda that the Nazi's used against the Jews is extensively recorded; placing Jews as vermin or a disease that the soldiers must eradicate.

Jehovah's Witnesses excel at this practice as they literally Demonize the Outside World; members are taught that Satan controls everything outside of the cult, and that members should not get involved with anything that is 'worldly'… like birthdays, holidays, or formal education. But you have to doff your cap to the Westboro Baptist Church, as they have built most of their ideology around Demonizing the Outside World; their poster-making department must go into meltdown every weekend! These protests really bring the cult together as one entity…

Quality 5: Group Allegiance

As you'll want your minion to see him or herself only in terms of your cult by losing their sense of Self (Discussed soon in Phase 5), creating a Group Allegiance against the Outside World will pull everyone in line; a kind of 'Circling the Wagons', so to speak. Each minion will identify themselves as part of the winning team, only if they stick together and work as one. This should inherently enforce conformity and squash any egos within the group; yours being the only ego that is allowed. This will also force the minions to make a very simple choice… some would say… too simple…

Quality 6: False Dichotomy

We will see in a moment that developing flawed thinking from common fallacies like '**False Dichotomies**' will break down a person's Critical Thinking skills but, in this instance, it does a whole lot more. **Demonizing the Outside World creates a binary landscape of 'Us v Them', forcing a minion to take sides, increasingly seeing themselves in terms of 'Us'**. The more they adopt the 'Us' as a personal identity, the more they will have to engage in acts of Cognitive Dissonance to justify the cult's actions, thereby normalizing the new life that they are leading. They will also need to defend the cult against, what will become seen as, unfair and unjust accusations by the Outside World; and a criticism of the cult will, effectively, become a criticism of the minion.

Robert Jay Lifton, an American psychiatrist and author explains it like this – "*The world [of cults] is sharply divided into the pure and impure, into the absolutely good and the absolutely evil. All 'taints' and 'poisons' which contribute to the existing state of impurity must be searched out and eliminated... once an individual person has experienced the Totalist polarization of good and evil, he has greater difficulty in regaining a more balanced inner sensitivity to the complexities of human morality.*"

Well said, Mr. Lifton. Well said.

This Demonization should initially be framed with sadness and regret that "*not everyone can be saved*". It's only when the recruit has Crossed the Bridge into the real cult that the bile and venom can be released. For that to happen, we need to step it up a gear…

Phase 4: Thought-Stopping Techniques

It is often said that only a fool would join a cult, but this doesn't really take into account what actually happens to a minion. As I pointed out in Phase 1, what a Cult Leader needs to do is find anyone who is feeling temporarily vulnerable (a TVT), and then slowly, step by step, switch off the Critical Thinking parts of the TVT's brain, as they develop a brand-new life within the cult, leading to a Complete Cognitive Collapse (CCC). Some might say that this is a terrible thing to do to a sentient human being… because it is, but it is necessary for a Cult Leader to succeed.

So, how is this done? There are 3 main techniques that will lead to CCC, - **Failure with Fallacies, Rhythmic Rituals,** and **Target Blindness.**

Technique 1: Failure with Fallacies

You should already be familiar with flawed thinking systems like **Circular Logic**, **Confirmation Bias**, **Cognitive Dissonance**, and **False Dichotomies**, and be using them against your minions at every chance you can get. There are, however, another two fallacies that you should have under your belt, that will royally screw with your minion's cognitive processes, rendering them malleable for you. This brings the total fallacies to **6**… **6**!

Pseudo Causality – a form of **non-sequitur** based upon Proctor Hoc (Latin for '*Because of this*'). This is when two or more unassociated events are given false connections, usually because they happen at the same time or soon after. So, if a minion is not behaving as they should, look to see if an accident or natural disaster has occurred recently somewhere in the world, and then blame the incident on the minion – "*That tornado has happened because of your negative energy! Those deaths are on you!*" ('Energy' is a good word to use as it has little specific meaning to most people and you can twist it to mean anything. I cover such useful language in Stage 5: Lesson 2, page 141)

Don't worry. As a Cult Leader, you won't need to validate the causal link between the two events, as your authority over your minions and Group Pressure will make them just accept the connection.

Apophenia is a flawed practice that stems from the human propensity to seek patterns in random information and images. The fact is, most humans are not very good at accurately assessing probability and chance phenomena; **something that the Gambling Industry makes a fortune from!** It's what leads people to shout - "*It's a sign! It was meant to be!*"

This can be a creative process, and can certainly be introduced to your minions as such, particularly when you are encouraging them to "*Open their minds to a whole new world of possibilities*". But you will eventually need to take a literal approach to it to break down their Critical Thinking. One approach can be to claim that a number has a vital effect on their lives – known as **Numerology**. The number 11 is a popular choice, favoured by Uri Geller[8] et al, but you can choose any random number you want and make everything fit around it. For example, you could choose the number **6**, and then make everything that you write about work within the number **6** (Please see the Contents Page… and all through this book). Over time, your minions will believe that the number **6** has great importance in all of the aspects of their lives.

Why would they do this? Studies have shown that the human brain 'filters out' much of the information that it receives from its different senses so that the conscious part doesn't get overloaded (*Martinez-Trujillo, McGill University*); we would struggle to survive in normal, every-day life if the brain didn't do this, particularly with social media! The important aspect of this fact is that the filtering system is flexible and ever-changing – often referred to as the **Cocktail Party Effect**, where a word or voice can change what is being filtered out. If you increase the importance of a number – or anything else for that matter – the brain's filter system for your minion will recalibrate to include the new values and beliefs that you are imposing on them. They will be forced to operate their **Confirmation Bias** to ignore the other numbers that they see, and only see what you have said is important.

---

[8] Uri Geller could have been a great Master. Unfortunately, he is too much of a nice guy and lacks the level of cruelty needed to be a successful Cult Leader. He is, however, intelligent enough to work within another industry that relies on subterfuge and coercion – Consumerism. He has many products, like crystal pyramids, that people can buy into.

Technique 2: Rhythmic Rituals

Whether it is through sound or movement - chanting, singing, drumming, dancing etc., any ceremony or exercise that involves repetitive rhythms can induce soft hypnotic, trance-like effects on the people involved, turning off the parts of the brain that engage in Critical Thinking; it could even just be a mass screaming session like the Raëlians practice… usually after an orgasm! This has been used for millennia but only recently understood in scientific terms.

Studies have shown that thought-stopping rituals like meditation can radically limit the activity within the… (take a deep breath) Posterior Superior Parietal Lobe (well done!), which is the part of the brain that deals with a person's orientation within space and time, (*D'Aquili & Newberg, 2000*). The study describes how, when this area is dampened, **the distinction between the self and non-self is broken down, leading to a blurring of the lines between reality and fantasy**; the perfect condition for molding someone.

The physical activity that often occurs with these rituals, particularly if breathing in and out quickly is encouraged (we're back to the orgasms!), creates a strong feeling of euphoria; not unlike a runner's high. Then this natural physiological after-effect can be sold to the minions as '*A Spiritually Awakening Experience*'. This process will run in tandem with the practice of Love Bombing, whereby reluctant recruits will be 'encouraged' to participate in a wondrous experience, and receive signals from the older experienced minions on how to behave.

The real kicker with this technique is that the minions, having experienced the event first hand, will take ownership of it and defend the experience from any outside criticism; after all, this was an experience that they ACTUALLY felt and lived… the fact that **it was simply a biological response to a physical activity that they were coerced into misinterpreting, won't occur to them!**

The effect should be repeated on a regular basis, even if the minions are on their own – Every Hare Krishna minion is taught to repeat the Hare Krishna mantras 100's of times a day.

Repetitive or discordant sounds can also trigger another version of Apophenia called **Audio Pareidolia**, whereby the minion may hear voices or harmonic patterns in the random noise that your minions will be making. It all adds to 'screwing with their brain'!

Technique 3: Target Blindness

Most people are goal and reward centric, addicted to any 'trophy', regardless of how minor it is; how many meaningless Gold Stars did you receive from a teacher or parent as a child?

The Computer Gaming Industry knows this, making billions from it, and every game has an almost never-ending number of challenges, with multiple level-ups; encouraging players to stay within the game, releasing dopamine after each 'Quest Completed'. Take a lesson from them and create lots of steps and stages, levels and phases for your minion to go through (Please see the Contents Page!). This can be in terms of their 'spiritual' development within your mythology, but it can also be done in their day-to-day lives with simple chores being given a great importance for them to get right; if they don't clean the floor in the right way (which will be decided by you anyway), get them to do it again… and again… until they are proud of cleaning a dirty floor 'the right way'.

The point is, you need to get your minions wrapped up in HOW they should be doing something, rather than WHY they should be doing it. They should be eager for that simple reward from pleasing you, waiting for the next chance to prove their vital worth from the meaningless targets that you have given them. From the simplest of tasks like washing, eating or sleeping properly, to really complicated life lessons that are ambiguous and ever-changing – like the Thetan Levels within Scientology, **creating a convoluted process of challenges for your minions will '*Keep their Eyes on the Prize*', preventing them from seeing the bigger picture… namely that you are a scam artist.**

The combination of these techniques, running in tandem with Peer Pressure, will really start to break down the cognitive processes of your minion. As I said before, they should be carried out gradually and repeatedly. Remember…

Repetition must be practiced at all times!

We have one more Phase to learn about before we can go for the jugular and make the minion Cross the Bridge into your cult…

Phase 5: Destroying the Self

A Cult Leader needs to see minions as just '*Cogs in a Machine*'; a machine that is there to serve the only ego in the room – namely, YOU! It is, therefore, illogical to allow minions to be competent, confident, independent individuals. It would make it nigh-on impossible for the Cult Leader to use and abuse them.

You'll, therefore, need to rid your minions of a sense of Self and any value given to independence. Some people might say that this is a heartless thing to do to an individual, empathic person… because it is, but a Cult Leader will fail if he doesn't do it.

So, how is it done? There are 3 main techniques that will lead to the destruction, - **Devalue Deduction, Self as Defective,** and **Remove Personal Markers.**

Technique 1: Devalue Deduction

The last thing that you'll want is for your minions to reach the reasonable conclusion, through logical thought processes, that you are full of doggy doo. So, along with the Thought-Stopping Techniques that we have discussed in Phase 4, you'll need to start belittling rationality and reasoning. This will be quite difficult, as most of your minions will see intelligence as a good thing, and will want to be clever… or at least be seen as such. So, you'll need to put a positive spin on Devaluing Deduction, and a sneaky trick for doing this is called - '**Appeal to the Unknown**'. This is when a Cult Leader tells his minions that they will be missing out on what is really going on in their lives if they only rely on logic and facts; "*You can't know the whole truth without going beyond what you know!*" This will make your minions believe that they have a greater understanding… whilst keeping them in the dark. Brilliant!

You could also use the twin brother of this trick – '**Appeal to the Unknowable**', whereby you explain to the minions that something is true, but that it cannot be known by mere mortals. . except you! A good example of this is from Happy Science, where Master Okawa, when talking about the many dimensions that exist, says – "*This is the most I can explain to you using words that you can understand. The Primordial Buddha of the great universe is most certainly the Being beyond the twentieth dimension.*" Excellent!

A different approach would be to encourage 'living the moment', and to avoid getting wrapped up in thought processes that could get in the way of reaching enlightenment. As Andreas would often explain to his Buddhafield minions – "*You need to 'Drop your Mind'. You don't want to be in the mind. No thoughts. If you're having thoughts, you're not connected to meditation and to God.*" He should receive a Gold Star for 'Embracing Hypocrisy'.

Another fun way of breaking down their reasoning skills is to play children's games, drawing out the child that is in all of us. There are several games that work well, like '*Musical Statues or Chairs*', '*I Spy*', or '*Simon Says*'... although you should swap your name for Simon to really reinforce your authority. Even giddily running around a forest, playing tag, will have the same effect.

These games can be presented as a group-bonding exercise, or as a relaxing psychological development program, but the key to them is that YOU will always be the one who decides who has won the game, regardless of the rules. This will take away the minion's ability to make decisions about the outcome, as there will be no fair way of playing it. These games will be very disarming and seen as non-threatening by your minions, even though they directly threaten their ability to think straight, as the lack of control over the outcome and the frustrations that will ensue, will force them to activate their **Cognitive Dissonance** in accepting the results.

Technique 2: Self as Defective

Most people see a healthy understanding of the Self as a vital part of their wellbeing, so if you say that they will need to get rid of it, they will selfishly go on the defensive. This means that you'll need to be far more insidious with your methods. I suggest that you take a leaf out of the Business sector.

As the old management mantra goes – "*If you want to get someone to do something, get them to want to do it first.*" So, in the same way that you can get people to give up their money by saying that 'money is the root of all evil', you can say that the minion's attachment to their flawed ego is what's preventing them from succeeding. They will be more than willing to rid themselves of what is holding them back.

But don't take my word for it. Shoko Asahara, who created the Aum Shinrikyo cult in Japan, described it perfectly when he told his minions that – "*In order to get rid of the ego, the Self must be disposed of as well. Humans love the 'Self', so they suffer. And if the 'Self' can be discarded, then a shining true Self will emerge.*" No 'truer' word was spoken, our Wondrous State-executed Sensei!

In many ways, this won't be a difficult sell, as the minions will have joined your Front Group because they already think that they are a pitiful excuse for a human being, but you'll really need to drive the message home for it to work; and I've got just the ticket for you to do this... **Systems of Disclosure**!

"*What is that, Professor Francis?*", I hear you ask.

Well, a Cult Leader can create a regular structure of Disclosure Sessions, whereby a minion will divulge personal failings and flaws - both past and present, under the guise of 'liberating' themselves from the chains of failure. This supposed 'Counselling Process' does, in fact, have a two-fold controlling effect.

Firstly, it serves to regularly remind the minion of how flawed they are, thus lowering their self-esteem... particularly when it is accompanied with a good dollop of condemnation and judgement, framed as "*I have to say these things or you won't improve!*"

Secondly, it gives the Cult Leader some bribing power over his minions for when he wants to threaten them or increase the High-Exit Costs (Discussed later in Stage 4). Perhaps someone talks about an affair that they've had, or corrupt business practices that they've carried out, or sexual encounters/orientations that they'd want to keep hidden. It all becomes 'useful' information for the Cult Leader to use and abuse.

If minions start to run out of bad things to focus on, you could always force them, through social expectation, to make things up. Indeed, by using the **Nocebo Effect**, you could actually convince your minions that they have more traumatic memories than they really have. **The Nocebo Effect is the evil twin of the Placebo Effect, whereby it can induce suffering through psychological suggestion** (*Benedetti, 2007*). Then you can apply the Placebo Effect to liberate them from the non-existent traumas. This will legitimize your authority to carry out the 'Counselling' procedure.

Again, Robert Lifton writes that one of the unique qualities of totalitarian systems like cults is that – "*There is the demand that one confesses to crimes one has not committed, to sinfulness that is artificially introduced, in the name of a cure that is arbitrarily imposed. Such demands are made possible not only by the ubiquitous human tendencies toward guilt and shame, but also by the need to give expression to these tendencies. In Totalist hands, confession becomes a means of exploiting, rather than offering solace for, these vulnerabilities.*"

Good observation, Mr. Lifton. Nice one!

The cult which best utilizes the **Systems of Disclosure** is Scientology, as it is central to its mythology that every human is flawed and grossly inadequate (it doesn't help having an invisible alien parasite attached to your back, controlling you, does it?) It's only through Scientology that minions can become 'Clear', and then later, become 'Operating Thetans'; free from those alien parasites to levitate and move objects with their mind… honest!

To get 'Clear', the minion must be 'audited' on a regular, sometimes daily, basis. Although these Auditing Sessions are framed as psychological support systems, they are, it is said, actually episodes of hypnotic suggestion, whereby minions are forced to repeat and focus on their failings and wrong-doings out loud, sometimes hundreds of times within a single session.

The cult keeps records on all of the minions, called Pre-Clear Folders, whereby all of their 'admissions' are recorded and then can be used against them as a form of character assassination or blackmail.

A case in point is Amy Scobee, who joined the cult when she was 14, back in 1978. When Amy eventually left, 27 years later, after working in the top levels of the organisation, the cult began running articles about her in its monthly magazine and on the internet, trying to discredit her, going into lurid detail of her sexual exploits as a young woman; information that was only attainable through her Pre-Clear folder. She later wrote about her experiences in her book, 'Abuse at the Top' – "*Unbelievably, I never blamed anyone for being put through these things. I just thought I needed to 'Confront it' and 'be tough and make it go right' We were so indoctrinated into believing that we're not our bodies, that the mission is more important than Self, and that anything personal can be easily sacrificed for the cause.*"

Now, she may not be totally discredited outside of the cult by these accusations, but most Scientology minions see her as evil and lost (now part of the 'Outside World'), and that's what matters. **They won't register her valid criticisms and observations**.

It's even rumoured that many of the big celebrity members of Scientology stay because they are fearful of the personal and 'sensitive' information, contained within their Pre-Clear Folders, being released to the media… Good… Good!

No matter how you do it, it's important for your minions to see the Self as something flawed and worth getting rid of for the cult's success. As Amy perfectly puts it – "*… anything personal can be easily sacrificed for the cause.*" Talking of something personal…

Technique 3: Remove Personal Markers

What makes you… you? Your name, your relationships, your profession, your hobbies, your interests, your style. Right?

Get rid of them all! I mean it!

Force your minions to rid themselves of everything that they once were. You should obviously frame it as '*moving on to a better place... blah, blah, blah*', but you want your minions to ONLY identify themselves as part of your cult; wrapping themselves up within it like a comfort blanket… as it slowly suffocates them.

So, start from the beginning. You can change the minion's name. Many cults do this; both Heaven's Gate and the Manson Family chose nicknames for the new members. Both Hare Krishna and Osho's cult, Rajneeshpuram, give Asian sounding names to the new members. **The point is to change the minion's name from their old, 'worldly' given name to something that is acceptable and identifiable to the cult, leaving their old identity behind.**

Any kind of change will do, but my favourite example is from the Damanhur cult[9] in Northern Italy, created by Oberto Airaudi in 1975. The new minions must change their names to something that is found in nature, like animals and plants. So, you can be guided around the great Temple of Humankind by a young woman called '*Ant Coriander*' (I'm not joking!), or you can buy merchandise in their shop from a woman called '*Sunset Butterfly Pineapple*' (seriously, Google it!)

Also, make sure that they demand that their family and friends use the new name, as that will really get their blood boiling; driving a wedge between them. This is because you'll need to get rid of them as well… unless they are willing to join your cult, of course. I will go into more detail on how to do that soon.

Your minions will need to find a new family and circle of friends within your cult. But a word of warning! You'll need to find a good balance between them being attached enough to these new loved ones to want to go through the 'hard times' to be with them, but then not too attached, in case one of them selfishly leaves, and then you'll have to force the minion to disconnect from them as well. I suggest that you should try to aim for the kind of superficial friendship that seems strong, but can be broken with little effort… you know… like the ones that people have on Facebook!

Then there is their profession and hobbies. If your minion has a good job, then you might want to keep them doing that, but with a good percentage of the wages going to the cult. If not, then suggest a career change and get them doing any jobs that will benefit you. Keep them busy doing different projects and tasks within the cult. Gradually, the time that the minion spends within the cult should increase, leaving less time for what they used to do. As this goes on, the cult should subtly suggest that certain hobbies and interests are good and that some are bad; waiting until the minion has Crossed the Bridge before it condemns and bans them outright.

---

[9] The Federation of Damanhur is a 'University of the Spirit', where positive thought, directing the best of people's energies, can achieve **a higher level of health and happiness for its members**. It's worth noting that the Leader, Oberto Airaudi, died in 2013 from Colon Cancer that had spread to his liver!

Then there is what they wear - '*Clothes maketh the man*'!

Get them all to wear the same outfits or uniforms, so that they have a singular, unified identity, seeing 'personal style' as arrogant. You could even get them to wear full head masks of your own image, like Asahara did in Japan, but I would say that this is going a touch too far… it's up to you!

The point of all of this is for the minions to <u>only</u> see themselves in terms of the Cult. Cult, Cult, Cult. Nothing but the Cult.

This way, they will become totally dependent on the Cult Leader for their well-being and happiness, setting them up for complete submission. As again, Chris Johnston explains in the documentary 'Holy Hell' (201**6**), after he had left Buddhafield – "*There's this social interplay that happens between highly co-dependent people and a pathological Narcissist. Who is going to give a person, who needs constant adoration and attention... who is going to give that to them ceaselessly? Somebody who relies on him as the source of their self-esteem.*" Spoken like a true minion, Chris! Well done.

So, there you have it.

3 Thought-stopping Techniques – Failure with Fallacies, Rhythmic Rituals and Target Blindness; and 3 techniques to Destroy the Self – Devalue Deduction, Self as Defective, and Remove Personal Markers... Wait! Wow! That makes **6** techniques in all.

6! **6** is everywhere in the Universe! Isn't that incredible?

If you think it is… then it's time to move on to the final Phase!

… and it's a doozy!

Phase 6: Isolation and Deprivation

This is the **6th** Phase (See, there it is again!) and it's really intense.

You may think that humans are immutable, sentient beings, with established views and opinions, and that they couldn't be changed personally beyond recognition…

You. Have. No. Idea!

It's remarkably easy to change someone, as long as you have built the groundwork beforehand, which is what the previous Phases have all been about. Oh, and you need to have an inordinate amount of narcissistic cruelty within you, but you should have that anyway if you want to be a successful Cult Leader. It's a given!

If you are operating a Compound Cult then the Isolation and Deprivation (IsoDep) will already be taking effect, although it doesn't hurt to have a barn or a basement within the Compound that can be seen as the 'Naughty Area', for when you really need to crush someone's spirit.

If you are operating a Closed or Open-Societal Cult, however, then you will definitely need to have a whole building or a complex (or in the case of Scientology, your own fleet of ships!) to create the environment for the IsoDep. These venues can be described as 'Rehabilitation Centres', or 'Dynamic Meditation Retreats', or 'Retraining Units', but they all need to be shut off from the rest of the world, including the other minions, so that you have complete and absolute control over the 'chosen few' who are being targeted.

The IsoDep will create a state of extreme physical and mental exhaustion, culminating in a Complete Cognitive Collapse (CCC). This collapse will be framed as a '*Spiritual Awakening*', and it's at this point that the recruit will Cross the Bridge to become a minion.

Hooray! A Gold Star for that minion!

And this change won't just happen at the physical or mental level; it will also happen at the genetic level! Recent, cutting-edge research by Prof. Tim Spector at King's College, London, is revealing that life-events can actually change the activity of our genes, switching them on and off - **The Science of Epigenetics**.

This means that if you create the right kind of oppressive environment, you can literally Genetically Modify your Minions to be predisposed to irrational thought and servitude. That's right! You can have your very own GMM's. Awesome!

How is this done? Well, the first consideration to understand is that you need to make the minion want to take the IsoDep process; it's a bit like making them give up their money or sense of Self. Again, it does force them to take ownership of the process, and also lessens the sense of cruelty that is being imposed on them, as they think that it will eventually be good for them if they succeed. But the real reason why you want them to think that they actually have a choice over the Isolation and Depravation, is to prevent the authorities, spurred on by the minion's interfering loved ones, from getting involved and 'rescuing' them.

If the minion states that they are choosing to be tortured and deprived, then there is little that the Outside World can do about it. **You will really escape some serious criminal accusations if the minion 'feels' that he or she is 'choosing' to have their freewill taken away from them!**

The second consideration, and this one seems counter-intuitive, is to limit the minion's time spent within the IsoDep process. Weird, huh? Well, if they go through the Cognitive Collapse for too long, then they will see the dangers of being outside the Cult as a better option than the trauma that they are going through inside it, and they will leave. What a waste of a potential minion!

In other words, you have to know when to release the pressure valve. It's better to periodically send a minion in and out of the IsoDep for a few weeks at a time, rather than keeping them in there for years, only to see them make a quick getaway, late at night. Think of it like this. Do you remember, back in Stage 1: Step **6**: Make Cruelty Your Best Friend (Page 41), where I told you that you needed to alternate cruelty with love to control someone? It's a bit like this with the IsoDep process. If you kept them in total degradation the whole time, then they would eventually leave; you've got to show them a bit of light at the end of the tunnel for them to have a false hope.

But what does Isolation and Deprivation actually look like?

Isolation

The Philosopher, Friedrich Nietzsche once said – "*If you gaze long enough into an abyss, the abyss will gaze back into you.*", so if you want your minions to become empty and vacuous, make them do empty and vacuous things, then they will 'become that which they have focused upon'.

Get them to stare at a blank wall for hours at a time, emptying themselves of any thoughts. Get them to repeat to themselves, hundreds of times in one sitting, vital mantras or teachings that you had just made up the night before. Get them to sit, silently, in a darkened room for a whole day but with other people around them, which will just add to their social anxieties and frustrations. Alternatively, get them to sit in the same darkened room, but play loud, noisy music or sounds for the whole day; that will really trigger the **Audio Pareidolia!** Get them to build something like a wardrobe or a bedstead and then take it apart, over and over again, until you decide that it has been built properly. You could refit your whole Compound this way!

All of the actions above, and more, can be framed as meditation techniques, or prayer practices, or psychological therapies, depending on your chosen theme. All of them, in reality, force the minions into their own bubble of existence, breaking down their cognitive and social abilities.

Studies have shown that, because humans are such social beings, and that they develop a sense of Self from these social interactions, when those interactions are prohibited for any length of time, the functioning of the brain breaks down; in some cases, even changing the structure of it (*Palinkas, Suedfeld, 2008*) So, make sure your 'chosen few' are isolated for long periods of time, with very little interaction with the other 'chosen few'.

Deprivation

You'll want your minion to be 'running on empty', so that they won't be able to resist the changes that are happening to them. When they are not doing their meditation/prayer/therapy practices mentioned above, they need to be working around the Compound, cleaning, painting, building… anything to keep them busy; busy, busy, busy. They should be surviving on about 3 to 4 hours of sleep a night. Study, meditation and housework. That's it!

Along with the lack of sleep, you'll need to reduce the amount of calorie intake for your minion; just a small amount of rice and vegetables, or some chunks of bread with water per day. You can present it as a healthy, 'natural' choice, free from the trappings of a decadent lifestyle, so that they can 'detoxify' themselves.

The combination of sleep and calorie deprivation will lead to your minion quickly becoming 'zombified', whereby they will just wake, work, conform and collapse back onto the floor to sleep… don't you dare give them a comfy bed to sleep in, all right!

The clearest way to understand the IsoDep process is to hear from someone who has been through it, first-hand. Shinichi Hosoi was a young cartoon animator when he joined Aum Shinrikyo in Japan in the 1990's. As he had trained to be an animator… he was given the task of welding machinery for the Sarin factories that Shoko Asahara needed to induce Armageddon, which seemed fair enough! (Remember: Don't give a date for the end of the world AND don't horde Sarin gas!!) This is what Shinichi told the author, Haruki Murakami, in his book 'Underground' – "*The work was hard, up to 16 hours a day. We were wiped out, and sometimes didn't get enough food. We didn't eat for two days once… I wasn't used to this kind of work myself, and got injured, burned, my face blackened, my glasses were falling apart. But no one ran away. 'This is all for the sake of enlightenment', I kept telling myself.*"
If Shinichi can understand the process, then so can you.

By the time that the minions get to the other end of the Bridge, they should be following orders by default, without the internal resources to think critically about their situation. They should be thanking you for the opportunity to be saved from a life of suffering and degradation… as they complete their umpteenth cupboard and nibble on a limp piece of lettuce.

Only then should they be released into the Cult as a fully-fledged minion. But, if they waiver at any point, back into the IsoDep it is!

Checklist for Stage 3

So, if you have faithfully followed the Phases that I've described, you should have found a non-threatening way of targeting the weak and vulnerable people in society, making money at the same time, perhaps by creating a yoga group or a self-help franchise.

You'll have gently guided your victims through the **6** Phases of Metamorphosis, understanding that some people take longer than others to complete the change; don't forget that you can use those differences to your advantage by saying that "*One minion isn't ready for the Truth, but another one is.*" - that should really get their competitive spirits racing, triggering their **Target Blindness**!

And you'll have saved a fortune in running costs by keeping everything to a bare minimum in terms of food, materials and power consumption; you could even get your victims to make the candles that will be the only light source for the rooms that you'll be keeping those same victims trapped in! Sorted!

If you have done all of those things, then you should have in your possession a group of irrational, compliant, and malleable minions; worshipping at your feet; hanging on your every word.

And the good news is that Cults are largely self-sustaining, as your minions will want to recruit and indoctrinate other minions; consciously to save them from a doomed future of course, but subconsciously to justify their own journey. They will do whatever they can to make the Cult a success because they absolutely, 100%, KNOW that they are doing the right thing. All that's largely left for you to do is sit back, make the occasional appearance, and fulfill all your darkest desires.

Is that it? Is the Cult completely set up? Well, no. As you'll see in Stage 4, there will be a need to increase the Levels of control for when there are any signs of rational thought, or any glimmers of independent resistance.

But, before we move on, I need to see if you have understood what I have taught you. Are you going to be able to carry out the **6** Phases of Metamorphosis properly?

Answer the next questions and I'LL decide if you are ready!

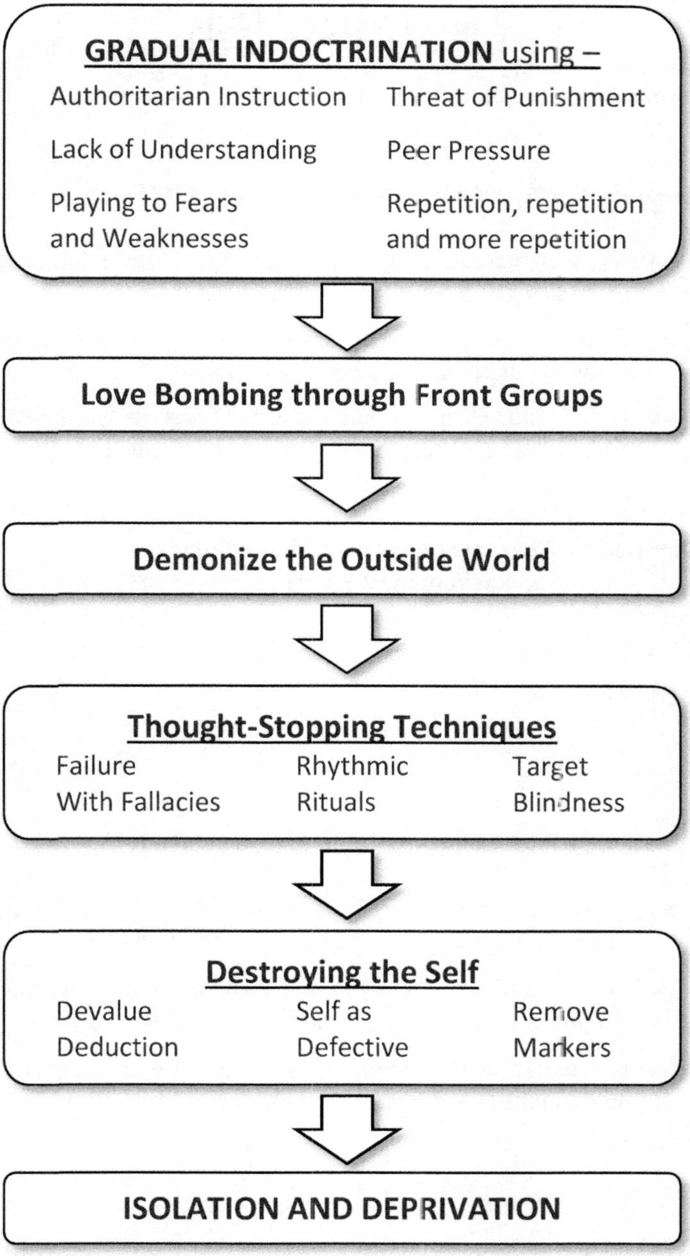
GRADUAL INDOCTRINATION using –
Authoritarian Instruction
Threat of Punishment
Lack of Understanding
Peer Pressure
Playing to Fears and Weaknesses
Repetition, repetition and more repetition
Love Bombing through Front Groups
Demonize the Outside World
Thought-Stopping Techniques
Failure With Fallacies
Rhythmic Rituals
Target Blindness
Destroying the Self
Devalue Deduction
Self as Defective
Remove Markers
ISOLATION AND DEPRIVATION

End of Stage 3 Quiz

Answer the questions below and see how you have scored.

Question 1) Why should a Cult operate a Front Group?

A) So that it can self-select vulnerable targets for the Cult, and make loads of money for me at the same time.

B) So that it can appear to be harmless, hiding in the shadows, ready to attack any unsuspecting victim!

C) It shouldn't. People should know what they are getting into from the start, so that they can make an informed choice.

Question 2) What must be practiced at all times so that Indoctrination can work?

A) Repetition.

B) Repetition.

C) Repetition.

Question 3) Why would you Demonize the Outside World?

A) It reinforces the Binary Landscape of 'Us v Them' in my minions, disabling their Critical Thinking skills.

B) So that I can threaten my minions with a doomed future by expulsion from my Cult, if they don't do as they are told.

C) I wouldn't, as it is unethical to manufacture an emotional and social conflict between people.

Question 4) How would you stop your minion from thinking?

A) I would give them lots of challenges to 'blind' them to what is really being done to them.

B) I would use 'Screaming Sessions' to emotionally drain them, overloading their senses and turning them to jelly.

C) I wouldn't. I would encourage individual expression and a healthy understanding of the Self.

Question 5) Which personal interests would you ban?

A) Only the ones that develop a sense of self-respect and personal development… so, all of them!

B) All of them! A minion's interest should ONLY be in me!

C) None. I would encourage a wide range of interests.

Question 6) How would you frame the IsoDep process?

A) "*It will bring such a clarity of understanding to your life. It's a wondrous experience that justifies the 'rough road'!*"

B) Frame? They do it, or they are doomed! Simple!

C) It's a series of abusive manipulations that are designed to break down an individual's autonomy.

How did you do?

Mostly A's – You are a right 'proper' Cult Leader. Stage 4 awaits.

Mostly B's – Almost! Just repeat the last Stage, **6** more times.

Mostly C's – Don't you understand that if you fail in becoming a Cult Leader, your life will be a disaster. You are doomed!

Stage Four:
Maintaining Your Minions

"Matters must be arranged in such a way that when the populace no longer believes, a prince can compel them to believe by force."

'The Prince' by Niccolò Machiavelli

Let's take stock and see how your journey is progressing -

Playing the part of a charismatic Cult Leader, and having created a vehicle for your desires, by now, you should have 'molded' some temporarily vulnerable and confused people into a group of wide-eyed, malleable minions, willing to blindly act on your command.

Job done, right? Wrong!

No matter how much you have disabled their thought processes, people have the irritating habit of experiencing moments of clarity that can really screw things up for you.

There are several reasons for this. It is true that, no matter how much you paralyze large chunks of the brain, remnants of rational thought will remain and 'fire off' just when you least expect it.

It's also possible that some loved ones of your minions, who aren't part of the Cult, could deviously concoct a namby-pamby social excuse for seeing the minion – like a birthday, anniversary or wedding. They could then remind that minion of what they used to be like, and of what their aspirations were, BEFORE they joined your Cult, annoyingly planting a seed of doubt into their minds about the journey that they are on. It's important to repeat: -

Always separate your minion from loved ones outside of the Cult!

Whatever the reason, there will come a time for most minions when, just for a moment, they will realize that you are full of crap and that your Cult is just a scam. What should you do when a minion has this moment of clarity?

Nothing! It's too late by then. You might as well shut up shop and go back to your pitiful day job. You have failed! You have failed yourself, and more importantly, you have failed me, your ONLY guide to a world of success and happiness. Thank you for wasting my time! You deserve to die, you worthless piece of turd!

Is this what you wanted to happen? Did you want to hear that?

No? Good. Then read on because you <u>are</u> worth it, and you <u>will</u> succeed. I have every confidence in your incredible capabilities.

(Did you see how the alternating 'cruelty and love' dynamic works; I bet you couldn't wait to turn the page over!)

My advice is to not wait until the moment of clarity occurs before you do something about it; be pro-active. You need to continually 'maintain your minions' by piling on Levels of oppressive control, so that when they have that moment of clarity, they will not feel ABLE to leave your Cult, even though they KNOW it is a scam. There should be such a High Level of Exit-Costs to leaving your Cult, that they will have no choice but to dig themselves ever deeper into their delusion. Over time, that clarity will be replaced with an even more fervent version of their devotion to you.

So, how is this done? As I mentioned back in Stage 1: Step **6** on page 41, the dynamic for a Cult Leader to mold his minions has direct parallels to the power and control that an abuser has over his partner (Battered Spouse Syndrome, BSS). We might as well, therefore, learn directly from the lessons in that social sector. Luckily, a small community in Minnesota have developed what is called '**The Duluth Model – The Wheel of Power and Control**', which shows all of the tactics and practices of such a dynamic. They have spent decades, since the 1980's, collaborating with victims and care workers to develop an ongoing source of support and understanding for both the victims of domestic abuse and the authorities that are trying to deal with such abuse… and we might as well take advantage of it too!

It is true to say that it is a 'work in progress', and they still have a lot to learn. For example, you can clearly see from the image below that the Spoke of the wheel that is close to 8 o'clock, is entitled '**Using Male Privilege**'… Well, duh! Everyone in the world knows that it is right that men should have male privileges. It goes without saying that we are '*Masters of the Castle*', yes? Also, you'll notice that the top two Spokes of the wheel are exactly the same as each other… just in very different ways. So, they might as well be considered to be one Spoke. This means that there are, in fact, just **6** Spokes to the Wheel of Power and Control. **6**! There it is again. The number **6** is everywhere! Unbelievable, right?

The Duluth Model: The Wheel of Power and Control

I will take each Spoke in turn and teach you how to pile on the pressure, using the tactics and techniques found within it.

Regularly come back to this page and refer to the image. Better still, go to the Domestic Abuse Intervention Programs (DAIP) website and get a clearer understanding of the Duluth Model; you will learn so much from it.

Work your way through the different Levels until they become second nature to you. Then you'll be able to relax, break away from the world of responsibilities, and reap your rewards.

Talking of 'breaking away from the world'…

Level 1: Disconnection from Loved Ones

Depending on the Cult Structure, the minion will already be experiencing a good dose of Isolation from the Outside World and this is a big key to controlling them. Scott Miller, a Batterer Intervention Specialist at the DAIP, explains the thoughts of an abuser – "*If I can control how she thinks, then I can control her. And the more contact she has outside of me, the less likely I'm going to be able to maintain that control.*"

So, although any kind of 'outside influence' will be bad, the main threat that you'll face is from family and friends who will actually care about the minion, unlike you. They are the arrogant ones who will dare to make an effort to prevent or save the minion from being abused by you… annoying bastards!

So, it is vital that you make your minion disconnect from any loved ones who are not in your Cult. There are two types of Disconnection, and they have two very different aspects to them.

The first type is the Disconnection from family and friends BEFORE the minion has Crossed the Bridge and joined the Cult. The problem comes from the fact that the family or friends won't have gone through the same **6** Phases of Metamorphosis that you have inflicted upon the minion. **Unlike the minion, they will be able to see the changes that you are putting the minion through, and because you haven't subjected them to the Thought-Stopping techniques that we have discussed, they will easily see through the doggy-doo that you are coming out with. So, the less contact with them the better.** If you are lucky, they won't know about all of the details of your Cult, and you can accuse them of being ignorant of what you are doing, framing the Disconnection to your minion as 'a necessary move to a better place, away from bad and harmful influences'. The Prophet Raël often explains to his Raëlian minions that - "*You cannot control who you were born to, but you can control who you build relationships with*", suggesting that it's good to disconnect from your family who are holding you back, so that you can progress through your difficult but wondrous journey… Then he starts a sex orgy again!

You're not going to be as lucky with the second type of Disconnection because it is the separation from family and friends who were WITHIN the Cult, and have been expelled or escaped.

This type of Disconnection has two factors to it. Firstly, the loved one who has left DOES know all about your Cult, and that is a real danger. They can create massive shock-waves that will disturb the other minions, spelling trouble for you. You'll need to immediately discredit them, and this is where '**Demonizing the Outside World**' comes into its own. The loved ones who have left must be seen as evil and doomed by the remaining minions. In fact, if you are doing it right, **your minions should see the deserter as worse than the other doomed people outside of the Cult because they DID know the Truth but have rejected it**. They are the worst of the worst and cannot be trusted. Anything they say should be regarded as a bunch of lies. That should save your bacon!

The other factor to this type of Disconnection is that it can be used as a threat in a couple of ways. If someone isn't toeing the line, they can be threatened with expulsion. Not only will they think that they'll be doomed by not being part of the Cult, they will be heartbroken to never see their family and friends again. Conformity restored! Likewise, and ironically, Disconnection can become part of the High Exit-Costs for a minion who is thinking of leaving and, in one way, would welcome being expelled, but would equally be fearful of losing everything in their lives. It is best described by Jeff Hawkins after he finally left Scientology in 2005, having spent nearly 3**6** years within the Cult – "*I had to walk away from a 35-year commitment; my wife who I loved very much; all of the friends I had in the world were at that Int. Base. A person has to be so desperate to just turn their back on everything, and say - 'I don't care about all that. I have to leave this place because it's just too oppressive', and walk out into a world that is just totally foreign, and where they don't know anybody. They don't know the rules. They don't know how to get a job. They don't know how to get a bank account. It's a foreign world and they have to go out and somehow cope with it, alone! And people say - 'Why don't they just walk out?' Well, that's why. Because, in essence, it's a kind of a suicide!*" Well done, Jeff. You understand that a minion needs to be completely dependent on the Cult…

Level 2: Enforced Dependency

"A wise Prince must find a way in which his citizens will consider him and his state to be indispensable in every circumstance and at all times. Then his citizens will be always faithful."

'The Prince' by Niccolò Machiavelli

As you can see from **Spoke 2** of the Duluth Wheel, controlling economic dependency is very important for an abuser, but for a Cult, it needs to go much further than that. The minions must believe that they are totally dependent upon the Cult for their happiness, for their morality, and for their future. They MUST believe that they couldn't survive without the Cult. As Jeff Hawkins said above, leaving a Cult is – "*a kind of a suicide!*".

So, yes, economically, you must limit or even take away the minion's ability to make money for themselves, depending on the structure of your Cult. If the structure allows, get them to close their personal bank accounts, having maxed out their credit first. They should 'donate' any property to the Cult. Don't give them wages as such (so that they don't have a work history for a CV), but provide an internal welfare system whereby they are given a small allowance to buy the basics and nothing else. Better still, do away with money altogether for your minions, and just provide the essentials directly to them upon request, like food, clothing and… well, what else do they need, for crying out loud? **This will allow your Cult to amass a fortune, whilst letting your minions believe that money is meaningless.**

Don't stop there. Make them socially dependent on the Cult. You'll have already got them to reject their old family and friends, and they will have no choice but to wrap themselves up within the new social structure of the Cult. If they think of leaving, they will need to consider what it would be like to start all over again. Finding a new partner, new friends and colleagues; losing contact with children. How scary is that for any of us at the best of times? Nigh-on impossible for a minion who isn't thinking clearly and had their sense of Self destroyed! Jeff Hawkins really did nail it!

But don't even stop there. Keep ramping up the pressure by making them intellectually dependent upon the Cult. By now, they will have stopped thinking for themselves anyway, but you need to continually remind them of how confused they would be without the Cult (**Embracing Hypocrisy** as you do so, of course); that they couldn't understand right from wrong without the Cult, as their ethics will have been thrown out of the window a long time ago; that they would end up stealing, killing and destroying everything around them without the Cult… OK, the last one would be a bit much, but you get the idea! Cult, Cult, Cult. Nothing but the Cult!

But don't even stop there either! You can make them dependent on the Cult for the most basic of things, like cooking, cleaning and sleeping. Give them strict schedules on how and when to do these elemental human practices. This shouldn't be strange or insulting for your minions, if you had made it part of the Though-Stopping Techniques, like I mentioned back on page 98 with 'Target Blindness'; they should be thankful to be told how to cut vegetables properly. Talking of which, if you are operating a Compound Cult, and all your minions are in one place, then compartmentalize all of the daily chores, and give one specific chore to each minion, with them only doing that one chore, over and over again. Why do this? Well, think of a person who lives on their own. They have to wash, cook, clean and plan for themselves. Even at this basic level, they get a sense of self-sufficiency. Strip even that from your minion!

Admittedly, this will all be easier to do within a Compound Cult, but you can still mirror many of the effects in the Closed and Open Societal Structures by getting the other minions to ensure that your instructions are carried out (Discussed more in Level 3 and 4).

There's no better way of describing it than by using the words of Vera Chieffo, who left Andreas and his Buddhafield Cult in 2009 – "*I did so much service for him, and didn't worry about the future, that when it was over, I had $45 to my name. I didn't have a bank account. I didn't have anything. I remembered just lying on the floor in a fetal position. It was like I was dropping through a trapdoor. It was black, and there was no bottom.*"

Ah! A minion in the fetal position. Is there a better sight than that?

Level 3: Social Echo Chambers

Controlling people in how they think and behave can be a tiring process and it would be useful to get other people to do the work for you. Luckily for us, there is a social phenomenon that can help. It's called a Social Echo Chamber, or as we call it in the Cult Trade – the **Duplicating Insular Systems of Communication (DISC).**

This is any form of enclosed transmission process that validates, reinforces and amplifies any belief or opinion, through repetition, with a deep distrust of contrary information – just watch Fox News!

As you will be limiting the minion's access to the Outside World, they will have no alternative but to turn inward for any stimulus. Each minion will be talking about what they have learnt with the other minions, wanting to keep 'on message' in order to receive the **Love Bombing** that is going around. Your messaging, opinions and instructions will be continually repeated by each minion, being validated and reinforced at every rendition; remember what I said in Stage 3 – "**Humans are hardwired to value repetition over reason**." This process will convert your fabricated nonsense into a factual view of the world for your minions, as they will stop listening to other possibilities and regard your repeated mantras as the ONLY TRUTH. The conversations should go like this –

Minion 1: "*Hi there. I have heard that the truth is X, Y, and Z and I agree with that.*" (nodding to Minion 2 for social approval).

Minion 2: "*Yes. I have also heard that the truth is X, Y, and Z and I also agree with that.*" (returning the nod of social approval).

Minion 1: "*Great. As we both agree about X, Y, and Z then it must be true. (*nod, nod*) Let's go and repeat it to the others.*"

This is clearly a flawed way of thinking, as many people can believe something to be true when it has been proven to be false – the Flat-Earth Movement springs to mind. But this is the point. You WANT your minions to operate a flawed social process so that it keeps them malleable and controlled. When you want to change your minion's record of the world, give them your DISC to play.

Ironically, at the same time as keeping your minions open to your whim and control, DISCs will close them off to other influences outside of the Cult, shielding them from potential interference from loved ones. As Donald Traill, the father of Stewart Traill, explained in some letters to the victims of the Church of Bible Understanding (COBU) – "*There is no earthly good entering into discussion with these people – or indeed any Fundamentalists – and the reason is simply that their minds are closed, 'insulated', as it were, against all contact with the world outside their own narrow circle of preconceptions.*" 'Insulated' indeed, Donald!

As long as your minions are seeing any outside opinion as dangerous and suspicious, which they should be doing if you've been Demonizing the Outside World (see how it all connects!), then they will reject outright those opinions or arguments, no matter how valid they are.

So, produce copious amounts of letters, books, magazines, DVD's, Private Internet Forums, Group Twitter Feeds – any kind of messaging that can be easily regurgitated between your minions. **It doesn't matter whether it is a physical 'Echo Chamber' or a virtual one, the result will be the same.** If you want to understand how powerful the internet can be in controlling a person's world view, just Google 'Incel Community'… You will be shocked!!

The other joy of this naturally occurring social practice is that, if you operate it properly, it becomes part of your ongoing coercion and intimidation processes, as a Social Echo Chamber is wholly based on conformity. It is self-policing against anyone who wants to try and speak out against the messaging. Have you ever heard of the phrase – "*He's trying to whistle into the wind.*"? Well, within a Social Echo Chamber, at the very least, a dissenter's voice gets drowned out. At the most, they get victimized into silence for trying to be different. Either way, dissension gets stamped out. Conformity is king. You can just sit back and watch them Groupthink their way into submission.

It's fantastic to get your own minions to police your own minions...

Level 4: The Surveillance State

Spoke 4 of the Duluth Wheel looks at how loved ones, especially children, can be used against the abused partner, and it's no different for a Cult. Yes, guilt can be utilized to control them, as we will see in the next Level, but you can also use loved ones to induce another emotional state in your minions that will aide in your control over them; **Paranoia**.

You'll need to make your Cult become a model Surveillance State, whereby you reward minions, especially family, who inform on other minions for not adhering to the rules and ideologies of the Cult. They must be willing to stab their loved ones in the back at the drop of a hat, framed, obviously, as defending the future of the Cult to save everyone inside – "*How can we protect all of us from poison, and also rid our loved ones of their poison, if we don't know who has been poisoned?*" This not only instills a crippling Level of anxiety into the minions, who will be too afraid to make a critical comment or a suggestion of defiance for fear of who may be listening and will 'sell them down the river', but it also creates a highly competitive environment, whereby each minion will try to seek favour with the Cult Leader by finding 'deviants' to sacrifice. They might even make things up about people just to get that reward (**Target Blindness**), which will really feed the paranoia.

This technique was used to great effect by Nazi Germany in World War II… and by Russia today. I suggest that you read up on the Stasi police in East Germany and learn about their tactics. If you can't be bothered to do all of that reading, poor you, then you can just watch the excellent film, 'The Lives of Others' (2006), and still get a good idea about what to do.

A minion's post or e-mails could be inspected, framed with '*an innocent person should have nothing to hide*'. You can certainly use whatever secrets you get in your 'Disclosure Sessions' to use as evidence of wrongdoing, even though you have promised that these sessions are completely 'confidential'. You could even go as far as some Cult Leaders have done, like Osho and Jim Jones, and put microphones everywhere to record what people are saying, but it's really about the 'feeling' of being scrutinized that is important.

As George Orwell wrote in his novel '1984' - "*You had to live – did live, from habit that became instinct – in the assumption that every sound you made was overheard, and, except in darkness, every movement scrutinized.*" **The minions must believe that they are being watched every moment of the day**.

But if one example from fiction won't convince you of the effectiveness of the Surveillance State, then how about an example from another work of fiction… Scientology! Jenna Miscavige Hill, the niece of the current Cult Leader, David Miscavige, described in her book 'Beyond Belief' the zeal with which most Scientology members would report on each other – "*Julia, in particular, became obsessed with enforcing the rules and checking people's mail.*" She then went on to write about how a 10-year-old boy was given the authority of a security guard to ensure that no one left a facility – "*He was only ten and about a foot shorter than me... it was downright disturbing how authoritative a little boy could be when given a little bit of power.*" You see? Jenna, who had been in Scientology from the age of two and left nearly twenty years later in 2005, saw first-hand how it can work, especially when children are used; they are really worth their weight in gold… but I'll go into more detail later about how children can be used.

The crucial factor about this Level is to get your minions to be eager to shop on their own loved ones (and anyone else) in order to protect the Cult, simultaneously knowing that their loved ones (and anyone else) will be eager to do exactly the same thing to them.

This practice of paranoia will really screw with their psyche!

Level 5: Guilt Trips and Traitors

As I mentioned in the previous Level, guilt can be used as a strong motivator in controlling someone. By making your minion feel that their failures and imperfections would not just affect their own lives, but the lives of their family, their friends, and the entire Cult, it really piles on the pressure to do what they are told.

Obviously, this is complete hokum as a single minion means nothing to a Cult, but the minions must believe that the future of the Cult is on their shoulders… pushing them down to their knees!

This may seem like we are giving them greater importance than they deserve, but you must know me by now; I would never give a minion a greater importance than they should have… if any at all! No. This false sense of importance is simply a ruse to demean and belittle the minion (see **spoke 5 of the Duluth Wheel**), as you can use their important 'responsibility' against them by continually questioning their ability to succeed. Point out their failings and humiliate them under the guise of making them stronger and ready for the challenges ahead (We've already covered this back in Stage 1: Step **6**: Make Cruelty your Best Friend on page 44).

It's a good idea to regularly question your minion's loyalty, which can become an insidious threat. You could ask – "*Would you want to let the Cult fail and destroy everyone's chances to find happiness?*" or "*Would you want to let your loved ones down by not following my path?*". Only use questions that have one answer – formerly known as **Leading Questions,** although we in the trade like to call them **Cul-de-Sac Questions**, as they lead the minion around in a little circle, back to the same point. It's the best kind of question to use on a minion as there is only one answer to give, thus negating the need for them to actually think about anything.

Guilt can also be used as part of the High Exit-Costs of a minion leaving a Cult. Not only will they never see their loved ones again, but the deserter, or traitor as it is better described, will put the whole Cult at the risk of failing. Again, this is a complete lie, but lying should never worry a Cult Leader. Additionally, by using the word 'traitor', you are creating a sense of loyalty within the other minions who do what they are told and don't even think of leaving. They will all want to be seen as loyal and do anything to prove it.

A good example of this technique is from Charles Manson and his Family. He would often ask his minions if they would be willing to do anything for him. Catherine Share, nicknamed Gypsy (remember to change the minion's name to help **Destroy the Self**), recalls a time when she was taken aside to witness a conversation between Manson and Clem (Steve Grogan). Manson asked if Clem would be willing to stop Gypsy from leaving the group by 'hunting her down, tying her up to a car and dragging her body along the ground slowly back to the ranch' – "*Would you do that for me, brother?*" Clem obviously agreed, as he didn't want to wrong his Master. Manson then turned to Gypsy and asked, "*Gypsy, are you going anywhere?*" Gypsy said 'No'. This may seem immoral… because it is, but minions see it as an admirable quality. So much so that, in this instance, Clem went on to father a child with Gypsy!

Can good people be this cruel? Yes, absolutely; both history and science tell us so. Studies have shown that, as long as you are seen as an authority figure, which should be the case as a Cult Leader, many people will go to almost any degree of cruelty to comply. The most famous study was from the 1960's carried out by **Professor Stanley Milgram**. He ran an experiment to test for conformity, although he pretended it was about a 'learning technique'. Two subjects were taken into a laboratory and asked to sit at a desk with electric controls. The genuine subject was to be the Teacher, and the other person – who was in on the experiment, pretended to be the Learner. The Learner was hooked up to electrodes in a concealed space and the Teacher would ask a series of printed questions. If the Learner gave a wrong answer, the Teacher had to press a button that supposedly gave an electric shock to the Learner (it didn't), and the Learner would fake being hurt. Each wrong question required the Teacher to turn the dial up to a higher degree of electric shock. The Teacher was urged, but never forced, to go on asking questions by the Experimenter (Authority Figure), even if the levels of electric shock would be at dangerous or fatal levels. They found that nearly **66**% of the subjects continued to the fatal level… **66**%! (The number **6** again!)

So, you can see that your minions will be as cruel as you want them to be. You just need to utilize that cruelty for your own aims.

Level 6: The Psychology of Previous Investment

Fortunately for Cult Leaders, human nature sometimes throws us a bone and assists us in our power and control over others.

Otherwise known as **Sunk Cost Fallacy**, humans will often continue with a course of action, even when they know it won't bring them any reward and cause a greater cost, purely because they have already invested so much time, energy, money, and emotion into it. The more they invest into something, the greater the Sunk Cost is, and the harder it becomes to admit that they have made a bad decision; **the high-end consumer industry is wholly dependent on this dynamic!** A Cult Leader can take advantage of this flaw as well.

Think about the minion who has rejected their own family and friends for your Cult, perhaps changing their lives completely. Think about how much money, time and effort they have invested in your Cult. Think about what they have sacrificed to be in your Cult, and you will realise how much the **Sunk Cost Fallacy** will help you in oppressing them. They will not want to admit that they were wrong all this time, particularly if they have defended you and your Cult against accusations of fraud from their loved ones. More often than not, most people will have no alternative but to operate their **Cognitive Dissonance** to continue with their flawed decisions, even when they know you are just a scam artist.

A rational person should forget about the costs incurred to date, and only consider the possible future costs and benefits. Fortunately for us, most people aren't rational.

The real joy of this Level is that, because it is part of their flawed thinking, you can blame the minion for staying in your Cult (See **Spoke 6** of the Duluth Model). You can answer accusations of abuse by saying – "*If you were being hurt so much, if it was so bad in our group, then why did you stay for so long?*" Level **6** allows you to blame the victim for what happened to them, even when there are genuine psychological explanations for their actions.

Checklist for Stage 4

Wow! It's been a long, tough journey but you've made it.

You have transformed yourself into a credible Leader, created a seductive Cult, found and gradually molded your minions, and now have created Levels of oppression to keep them caged, even when they have realized that it is all a scam and you are just a liar who is abusing them for your own benefit. Brilliant! Well done!

But is this the end of the book? Is this the end of my help?

Of course not! I don't do things by half measures!

There are still some Vital Lessons in a Cult Leader's Life to be learnt; some pitfalls to avoid; some tricks of the trade to utilize so that you can reach your full potential. You have invested so much in this journey that it is only fair that you get your money's worth. You should benefit fully from my knowledge so that you can reach perfection. You'd want to be the perfect Cult Leader, wouldn't you? Other Cult Leaders discover these Lessons through trial and error, tripping over them as they stumble through their journey.

You, dear reader, will be handed these Lessons on a silver platter.

But before I hand that silver platter to you, I need to know if you have properly invested the time and energy into learning these words of wisdom.

Answer the following questions and I'll see if I am the one who has wasted his time. Let's see if I should invest any more of my know-how on you.

End of Stage 4 Quiz

Answer the questions below and see how you have scored.

Question 1) Why would someone leave their loved ones, just to be in your Cult?

A) I have enlightened them to the fact that they won't be happy if they don't let go of their corrupt past!

B) They have realized how disruptive and corruptive the loved ones are… as I clearly explained it to them!

C) They were unaware that they've been subjected to systematic changes to their personality and world-view.

Question 2) What is the point of designating the same specific chores to your minions all of the time?

A) They forget any skills that they could use outside of the Cult.

B) They lose confidence and learn their place within my Cult.

C) There isn't any. People should have a wide range of skills and abilities in order to be independent individuals.

Question 3) What are the main advantages of Duplicating Insular Systems of Communication (DISC)?

A) A DISC is easy to set up and is largely self-sustaining.

B) Social Echo Chambers validate and amplify my fabricated doggy doo. Lovely!

C) There are none. Anyone who wants a balanced, contented life should explore a broad spectrum of views and opinions.

Question 4) How would you make your minion feel that they were being watched?

A) I would say aliens are watching them, day and night.

B) I would publicly reward minions for snitching on others.

C) I wouldn't. I would encourage people to value 'private spaces and times' to develop a healthy sense of well-being.

Question 5) When would you incite a group retribution?

A) Whenever I heard doubt or dissension.

B) Randomly, to create even greater guilt and anxiety!

C) Never, as it could lead to discrimination and violence.

Question 6) Why would someone stay in an abusive Cult?

A) Because they see it as a test of their worthiness.

B) They want it! They deserve it! It's their fault!

C) They have lost contact with the very loved ones who would forgive them for making a very understandable mistake.

How did you do?

Mostly A's – You're almost the perfect Cult Leader. Stage 5 will make all of the difference. Keep going!

Mostly B's – You're almost getting it, but it is possible that you could end up in prison! Read the book again, a few more times.

Mostly C's – Why do I bother with you? You are a waste of time!

Stage Five: Vital Lessons In Life

Lesson 1: The Persecution Principle

If you are being an effective Cult Leader, you will begin to see quite a bit of antagonism from various sources; the loved ones who have lost somebody to your Cult, the traitorous ex-minions who have left your Cult, and from the local authorities who have been emotionally blackmailed into action by those same sniveling loved ones and traitors who have realized that you are a charlatan! Meddling Fools! It can all be a bit unsettling for a new Cult Leader, who may worry that it could disturb their future happiness.

Don't worry. I've got some calming advice to give to you. Being socially persecuted and hated can actually be a good thing! **Nothing builds group cohesion like a good dose of Outside Persecution; it really 'rallies the troops'!**

As an example, consider the Westboro Baptist Church, infamous for their 'God Hates Fags' campaigns, where they picket the funerals of the dead, and decry America as doomed for its embrace of homosexuality. They have used the media to effectively vilify themselves to the entire American nation (and elsewhere). But this is exactly what Fred Phelps wanted. He even wrote the vilification into his sermons, predicting that they would be hated for 'speaking the truth'.

When their vile actions naturally provoked a reaction, Phelps would point to the fact that he had predicted it. This would validate his authority and unite the Cult even more. The ever-increasing number of minions who have left the Cult report that there is an omnipresent feeling of being attacked by the Outside World, and that this feeling has engendered strong social ties within it. This is an excellent example of how to operate The Persecution Principle.

If you don't like the idea of spreading hate… what are you doing becoming a Cult Leader? But, if you don't want to openly 'appear' to be spreading hate, then you could still get the same unifying effect… by faking an assassination attempt on yourself, which is what Jim Jones did in 1972. He was trying to rally his Peoples Temple minions to buy properties in San Francisco and Los Angeles, but they were much happier staying in Redwood Valley. So, he spent a few weeks saying that he had received some death threats. Then he got a couple of his trusty Supporting Witnesses to put a few holes in a shirt, stain it with blood, and then fire a gun with blanks at the minions whilst they were having a picnic. In the confusion, Jones pretended to be shot and fell to the floor. Everyone ran for their lives into the church, frightened out of their wits and horrified that their 'Father' had been shot. A little while later, a Supporting Witness walked in with the 'blooded' shirt that had 'bullet holes' in it, and then, as if by magic, Jones walked in, healthy and stronger than ever. He had cured himself of being shot! The stunt taught the minions that they should move to a safer place and they left Redwood Valley soon after! Jim Jones used The Persecution Principle not only to unify his minions into conformity, but to also provide proof that he was immortal. Genius!

Leading on from this, The Persecution Principle can also be used to trigger a defense mechanism within your minions in case you really are being set upon by any critic. By now, the minions should see themselves 'as one' with your Cult, so a criticism of the Cult will be taken as a personal attack on them. They should perceive it as a real harmful threat. Their survival instincts should kick in with an adrenalin rush and accelerated breathing; ready for a fight. **Their physiological reaction should be overly disproportionate to the verbal criticism; this kind of overt reaction is a good Litmus test to see if they are being 'proper' little minions**. Imagine for a moment, the picture of an ant's nest that has just been disturbed – Soldier ants frantically rushing around, attacking anything that comes near. To paraphrase Shakespeare, The Persecution Principle will make your minions '*stiffen the sinews, summon up the blood, and make them want to kick the crap out of anyone who questions you*'!

A word of warning! Be careful with how far you take this aspect of the principal; there is a tendency for it to get out of control. Consider the case of the Temple of Love Cult[10], led by Yahweh Ben Yahweh (his name before the **Transformational Epiphany** was Hulon Mitchell Jr). Whenever he saw people as a threat to his authority, which was quite often, he would automatically operate The Persecution Principle… and get his minions to kill the person. The trouble is, as I'll explain later in Lesson 5, killing lots of people tends to get the authorities involved, and it wasn't long before the 'Architect of the Universe' - (don't forget to give yourself a **False Title of Importance**) – was locked up in prison, later dying from prostate cancer. So, yeah, be careful with this one!

Instead of using The Persecution Principle for serial murder, you could rein it in a bit and use it to just discredit the people who are criticizing you. You can suggest that they have an 'ulterior motive' for 'spreading lies' against you, and that you are the victim of 'fake news'; people are reluctant to criticize a victim. This is formerly known as **Ad Hominem** (Latin for '*to the person*') and it's a common fallacy used when the criticism cannot be fairly rebuked… usually because it is perfectly valid. So, the only response is to use misdirection and criticize the 'troublemaker' instead, or as we like to say in the trade – '**Misdirect to deflect**'! Never be afraid to place yourself as the injured party in order to dodge some awkward questions or accountability, even when it is clear to everyone that you are in the wrong.

Finally, The Persecution Principle could allow you some privileges above other groups, as victims generally need greater support than others. You might even be able to claim for financial compensation from your fabricated discrimination.

All in all, The Persecution Principle is a very useful social tool. Whether it is to unite your Cult, avoid criticism, gain privileges… or to prove that you are immortal, you should have the Persecution Principle as a default setting.

---

[10] Getting minions of a Cult called 'Temple of Love' to decapitate and beat people to a pulp is an extreme interpretation of 'Embracing Hypocrisy' – not one that I would recommend!

Lesson 2: Media Management

As a Cult Leader, you need to understand the power of words and images. Simple semantics can make the difference between being seen as a deranged Cult, hell-bent on stealing young people, or having a spiritually rewarding religion, that attracts big-name stars and tax-exempt government status.

The most important thing is that you have control over how your images are used and what you 'say' that you have said. This is very difficult to do in the modern digital age of multimedia. Back in the day, if you could control the newspapers, you could pretty much control what the public thought. It's not so easy now. This is why I recommend that you don't really engage with the media, beyond your own internet forums, webpages and tweet chambers.

Scientology tried to control the media for a time but, as I'll explain later, it didn't go so well. David Miscavige, and other 'frontline staff', have not been seen in the media for years. And most other Cults don't bother either. I suggest that you follow suit.

If you do decide to publicly engage with the Outside World, there are a few tips that can help you.

Firstly, it may seem obvious, but it's important that you never describe your Cult as a Cult. Unfortunately, Cultism has got itself a bad reputation over the years, just because of a few bad apples… like Charles Manson, David Berg, Jim Jones, Joseph Di Mambro, Marshall Applewhite, David Koresh, Warren Jeffs, Stewart Traill, James Gomez, L Ron Hubbard, Shoko Asahara, Ervil LeBaron, Credonia Mwerinde, Yahweh Ben Yahweh, Ron Lafferty, Osho, Hon-Ming Chen, and Sun-Myung Moon… to name but a few.

So, you don't want to be tarnished with their 'mistakes'. The chosen Cult Theme will guide you to what you should call it. A religious 'sect or community' will bring an immediate legitimacy to your Cult, but in the modern world, a 'spiritual organization', 'philosophical movement', or 'social campaign group' now has pretty much the same public status… only without the tax relief.

It's up to you. Just don't call yourself a Cult; people who could easily buy into your boloney would avoid a 'Cult' each time.

The second tip, especially where language is concerned, is that 'detail is your enemy', particularly when dealing with the Outside World. You can get as detailed as you want with your minions because you have broken down their Critical Thinking skills. You can contradict yourself all the time and their **Cognitive Dissonance** will plaster over any gaping holes in your lies. Not so with the Outside World; they'll see right through those holes.

So, keep things vague and ambiguous. Use generic phrases and words that can mean anything and can be interpreted in different ways. Words like 'energy', 'aura', 'cosmic', 'spiritual', 'wellness', and 'essence' all have specific meanings, but have been used out of context for so long, that they have become plastic enough to be virtually meaningless to most people. For example, Shoko Asahara would say – "*The world of spirit is virtually boundless. The treasures you can find there are priceless and the reward is great.*" Or from Scientology's own website – "*Man is a spiritual being endowed with abilities well beyond those, which he normally envisions.*" Doesn't that all sound really meaningful... without actually meaning anything? By using these kinds of words and phrases, if someone questions you on a specific point, you can easily patronize them and say that <u>they</u> are the ones who are confused and don't understand the context of which you are using; that it is <u>their</u> ignorance that is blinding them to the truth. This puts them in the defensive position and maintains your authority. It's very easy and useful to utilize an **Ad Hominem** when using this kind of language (mentioned before in Lesson 1).

Along with generic language, a third tip is to use lots of metaphors, allegories, and symbolism, when describing your truth. Again, it allows them to mean anything you want them to mean, but it does something else. When you are dealing with the Outside World, they are metaphors, etc., but with your minions, the trick is to make them take it literally, as it will force them to operate their **Cognitive Dissonance** to take the bizarre descriptions as real.

For example, when Ryuho Okawa describes how humans came to be on Earth, he says that the Venusians (Beings from Venus... I'm not kidding!) invited other beings to join them on the planet - "*The first humanoids invited were from planets in the Magellanic Clouds, a rather self-assertive, egocentric, and combative type of race... they had the unique characteristics of pointed ears and feline tails.*" If someone from the Outside World questions it (as anyone rightly would!), he explains that it is all 'symbolism'. Bullet dodged! His Happy Science minions, however, have to take it as a 'literal account'. This not only erodes the minion's thinking skills further, but it increases the High Exit-Costs for the minion, as they would have to admit to people that they believed in all of this rubbish (as discussed before in Stage 2: Part 5: Motivational Mythology: The Fantastic Rule, page 70). It really does work. **Come up with some crazy stuff and say that it's a metaphor!**

Things have sadly changed for Cult Leaders over the last few decades. It used to be easy to deny any claims made against them. Now, with the Internet and digital technology, there is almost a constant record of what is being said and done; everyone has a bloody camera in their damn smart phones, and they tend to download it straight away (sometimes in real time) onto YouTube or Facebook! This is one of the reasons for the declining membership of Scientology. You can easily find YouTube clips of former Public Relations Manager, Tommy Davis, denying that Scientology has a 'Disconnection' policy, yet other videos show him confirming that they use that very same policy. When some female minions went on live television to defend David Miscavige from accusations of violence and abuse, they came across as a bit creepy and 'Stepford Wives-y'. When Tom Cruise did a promotional video, expressing his thoughts on Scientology... well, just go on YouTube and see for yourself... not good! Along with the numerous internet exposes, and Leah Remini's in-depth and ongoing TV series about Scientology, the Cult is losing control over its public persona. Even with its formidable resources, it's losing the battle and it's having an effect on its minion numbers.

The Lessons are simple. Keep media contact to a minimum. Don't let yourself be filmed. Don't let your speeches end up on the Internet, unless you're using empty rhetoric. And if anyone from the media contacts you, just tell them the truth: You are a small sect of like-minded brothers and sisters, worshipping your God...
...leave out the part that you are the reincarnation of Jesus Christ!

Lesson 3: Accounting for Authorities

Dealing with the authorities can be a tricky business. Humans can become pretty upset when their loved ones disappear out of their lives and re-emerge on a farm in rural Utah, exclaiming that they no longer want to play a part in a corrupt world, that they have given away all their money and possessions, and that they will devote the rest of their lives to their new 'Cosmic Master'.

In these circumstances, humans tend to make an effort to get the authorities involved! Annoying, aren't they?

It's worth remembering though that the degree of hassle that you can anticipate from the authorities will largely depend on three factors. 1) How much your Cult mirrors other, more mainstream, faith-based organizations. 2) The popularity of your Cult. 3) The number of extreme behaviours, practices or tenets found within it.

For example, if your Cult is borrowing much of the template from Mormonism, like the House of Aaron or the Apostolic United Brethren, then you'll tend to find little attention from the Outside World… as long as you don't marry off the children to the adults! If, however, you've created a Cult based around Vampirism, then phone calls might be made. Even then though, as long as you've only got a few dozen minions who are giving themselves over to the Dark Side by dancing naked around a camp fire in some remote farmland, those phone calls will largely be ignored by the authorities. If, however, you have over 100,000 Vampire minions, all dancing naked around campfires across the whole country… let's face it, the phone calls will get a response. And if those Vampire minions pour the blood of sacrificed goats over their children as they dance naked around the campfires, then the phones are going to melt and the police sirens are going to start wailing!

So, if you think that your Cult will not be able to hide behind the shadows of other faith-based groups, and that your practices will cause some 'attention', then there are some tactics that you can utilize to deal with the authorities.

The Best Defense is a Strong Offence

Going on the attack is one strategy, although, as you will see later, it shouldn't be a physical violent attack!

Scientology found itself on the receiving end of what it claimed to be 'persecution' - (always operate **The Persecution Principle**), when, back in the 1970's, the Federal U.S. Government dared to investigate the Cult for abuse and tax evasion. Thus, Operation: Snow White was initiated by a department of the Cult called the Office of Special Affairs (OSA), formerly the Guardian's Office.

Operation: Snow White consisted of deep cover infiltrations and organizational theft of documents from over 13**6** government agencies. Parallel to this, Scientology began a Terror Campaign against several top officials within the Internal Revenue Service, alongside an avalanche of lawsuits meant to cripple several specific government agencies. While an FBI investigation did result in sending eleven highly-placed executives of Scientology to prison – including L Ron Hubbard's third wife, Mary Sue, the operation was largely successful as the government essentially backed away from investigating the Cult and granted it tax-exempt status.

While this battle was occurring with the Federal Government, Scientology was also waging a war with the local city government in Clearwater, Florida, where they had based their operations at the time. This was a much easier fight for them, as they flooded the local elections with their own candidates (with heavy financial support) and eventually ended up co-opting the local government, thus permanently closing any investigation by the local authorities into the Cult's actions. Hooray!

Interestingly, Osho's Cult in America, Rajneeshpuram, tried to do a similar thing by taking over the local authority of the town that they had settled in, Antelope in Oregon. This was starting to work, but they got greedy and tried to take over the whole county without having the necessary clout and influence to do so. They resorted to trying to poison potential negative voters by putting salmonella in the local cafes, just before the elections. It all went horribly wrong when a criminal investigation led to the minions involved being imprisoned and Osho agreeing to be deported. Boo!!

The Lesson is clear – Only attack if you can see it through.

Bribery Will Get You Everywhere

Let's be honest. Money talks, doesn't it! Sun Myung Moon knew this because he donated so much of it to the American Republican Party that he was a VIP guest at the Reagan/Bush inauguration. These campaign donations have continued up until the present day and many high-level Republican operatives have regularly been spotted at Moonie events, such as the mass weddings. In addition to the campaign donations, Reverend Moon started one of Washington D.C.'s most prestigious political newspapers, *The Washington Times*, which can push out any old Moonie messaging. It is still owned by the Cult through 'Operation Holdings'.

All of which gave Sun Myung Moon considerable legitimacy and political clout within America and around the world. So much so, that he was given several contracts within the Department of Homeland Security… which is quite amazing, given that he had been convicted of tax fraud in the early 1980's, and had gone on record, offering very strong anti-American propaganda.

But that's the lesson. Words are cheap and can easily be bought!

Wave Goodbye to Your Troubles

A self-imposed exile can seem like 'cowardly spinelessness'… because it is, but it does have its uses. For example, fearing the authorities would arrest him for his prolific paedophilia, David Berg changed the name of his Cult from 'Children of God' to 'The Family of Love' (later renamed as 'Family International'), and escaped to numerous compounds that he owned around the world, moving regularly. This made it almost impossible to build a case against him because of the ever-changing jurisdictions, by-laws and legal hurdles. He died, still in exile, in Portugal in 1994. The authorities never arrested him, so the exile thing kind of worked!

The lesson is, although you don't have to do it for a lifetime, sometimes laying low for a few years or even decades, can let the proverbial heat calm down, allowing you to carry on with your path - '*He who runs away can live to screw people over another day*'… or something like that. Besides, having your minions know that you are 'persecuted' and unable to be with them is a great way to engender a frustrated form of attachment to loss - '*Absence makes the heart grow wonder*'… or something like that.

Lesson 4: Influential Innocence

If your aim of creating a Cult is to get people to show absolute devotion and adulation to you, then it can be fair to say that you'll want to limit the number of children being born into your Cult; nothing makes someone lose focus like a giggling baby! You can, of course, force your male minions to have a vasectomy or force your female minions to have an abortion (Heaven's Gate and Buddhafield, respectively) but that tends to get the authorities involved and, as we have seen, that's not necessarily a good thing. So, telling your minions that "*sex will hinder their righteous journey*" should limit the production of little ankle-biters.

But I do feel that it is my duty as your 'One True Guide' on your path to happiness that, if you do this, you are really missing out on a wonderful, special gift. Not the gift of life... that is worthless, but the gift of a Ready-Made-Minion, otherwise known as a child.

There are some fabulous benefits from having lots of children within your Cult, and although some people might find this a 'sensitive subject' (Snowflakes!), it's worth exploring carefully.

Firstly, as I mentioned, children are naturally pliable and compliant; **they are primed to follow adult control by nature**. Children will not only believe ANYTHING that you tell them, but they will wrap those beliefs up into their own identity. You don't have to worry about '**Destroying the Self**'; the process happens automatically. This is why getting minions when they are young, preferably from birth, is so important for a Cult.

Secondly, children have an inherent perception of innocence by others, which makes them great fund-raisers and recruiters for your Cult. Most people may be deeply suspicious of giving money to an adult who is coming out with your made-up crap, but those same skeptics tend to melt into submission when approached by a doe-eyed child. Sun Myong-Moon knew this when he said – "*Before children, even the most cynical people throw down their masks...*" Having a child preacher in your Cult can increase your financial donations by up to **66**%![11]

---

[11] This is a fabricated statistic, but don't be afraid to make this stuff up. People buy into claims more readily when supported by 'stats', but rarely verify them.

A word of warning! Keep a tight rein on these child preachers. As they are so committed to their delusion, they have a tendency to 'run with it' and take their own path, which, as we'll see in the next Lesson, can be dangerous for the current Cult Leader. Both Jim Jones and David Koresh were child preachers before they struck out on their own, taking many minions with them. So, be careful!

The third benefit to having children in your Cult is that they can be a useful front or buffer when dealing with critics and protestors. The Westboro Baptist Church uses this advantage to great effect. They will say the most vile and offensive things, calling dead soldiers at their funerals a 'retribution from God', and then put their own children at the front of the oncoming reaction. Cheeky!

Another benefit is that nosey authorities have a bit of a taboo over interfering with the parent/child relationship. You are welcome to 'home tutor' your children into prejudice, bigotry and ignorance - punishing them how you see fit, and the authorities will hesitate to the point of stagnant apathy to do anything about it.

Also, children can be very useful as part of the High Exit-Costs when dealing with a doubting parent within your Cult: "*How would you feel if you never saw your children ever again?*" is normally enough to quash any criticism or hesitation. Nice!

Finally, and most obviously, instead of having to go out looking for minions, you can stay at home and make them; many Cult Leaders have had lots of children with different women – Sun Myung Moon = 12, Shoko Asahara = 12, Fred Phelps = 13, and David Berg = ?... actually, it's difficult to know the final figure with David... not without DNA testing, anyway! Now, you certainly won't need to go to the lengths that Anne Hamilton-Byrne did back in the 1970's in Australia. Her Cult, The Family, arranged disadvantaged children to be 'redirected', otherwise known as stolen, from a psychiatric hospital that one of the minions ran, and carted them off to her Compound near Melbourne. This, naturally, brought her to the interest of the authorities and, after a long legal battle, she was fined and had the children taken away from her. A waste of time and money! Just stay at home and make them!

From womb to tomb, children are the most committed minions a Cult Leader could hope to have. Make lots of them!

Lesson 5: Death and the Afterlife

Many Cults like Peoples Temple, Heaven's Gate, and Order of the Solar Temple have ended in mass suicide. Many Cults like Peoples Temple, Aum Shinrikyo, Temple of Love, and the Manson Family have killed innocent people from outside the Cult.

I want to make it absolutely clear that this kind of behaviour is completely and utterly wrong.

Wrong, wrong, wrong! Don't do it!

It is so counter-productive! Seriously!!

In the case of mass suicide, why go to all the bother of setting up your Cult with multiple Front Groups and countless seminars and workshops, if you're just going to order everyone to permanently 'leave you'? You're going to have to start all over again. It's just pointless! Even worse, you might get caught up in the moment and commit suicide yourself. This is what happens when you believe in your own lies, and you should never do that; it's a bit like a drug dealer taking his own drugs. A disaster waiting to happen! I want you to repeat this mantra **6** times in the morning and **6** times before you go to bed – "*My pants are on fire, 'cos I'm a pathological liar!*". This should keep you grounded.

In the case of murder, it may seem like a good idea at the time to kill someone who is bothering you but, as I'll explain later, it just makes things a whole lot worse. It simply isn't worth it. OK?

Mass Suicide

While I strenuously condemn mass suicide, at the same time, I can understand why it can happen. Who among us have not got a bit carried away with our own prophecies, right? It's the equivalent of a soldier who has been preparing for years to fight in a battle, and then if it doesn't happen, he goes to the nearest town, looking for a fight. The difference is, when your daily 'bread and butter' is preparing for Armageddon, things can get seriously out of hand. You need to be extra vigilant and disciplined with this one.

I could give you numerous examples of this dynamic, and the tragedies of Peoples Temple, Heaven's Gate, and the Branch Davidian's demise at Waco are well documented, but I'd like to reference a slightly more obscure Cult that has all of the same hallmarks with this issue.

Consider the case of 'The Movement for the Restoration of the Ten Commandments of God' (I wish they'd have come up with a snappier name for their Cult, but there it is!), created by Credonia Mwerinde and Joseph Kibwetere

In Uganda, back in the 1980's, Credonia Mwerinde was a prostitute and in trouble with the law for theft and arson. Then, one day whilst in a cave, a vision of the Virgin Mary came to her in the form of a rock that looked a bit like a human (using Pareidolia to help her create her **Transformational Epiphany**[12]). Mwerinde was certain that she was having these visions (**Always be Certain**) and tried to convince other people that the rock had spoken to her, and was doing so with greater frequency, but it was a hard sell. Luckily for her, she met Joseph Kibwetere, a Roman Catholic former politician, who had greater clout with the public. He also started saying that he knew of those vision from the Virgin Mary and the two joined forces creating the aforementioned 'Movement for the Restora… yadda yadda yadda'! Their Cult grew and they built schools, churches and homes in poor, rural areas of Uganda, targeting the needy. They obviously built a bigger, more luxurious home for themselves (**Embrace Hypocrisy**). The pair took on a similar dynamic to Applewhite and Nettles in Heaven's Gate, but the roles were reversed; Mwerinde had the visions (Messiah) and Kibwetere interpreted what they meant (Soothsayer). The important thing was that she was the only person to receive these visions (**Be the One and Only**). To begin with, her messages were of 'humble guidance to a better world' (**Project Humble Righteousness**), but over time, her visions took on a more apocalyptic fervor (**Doomsday Device**), and people had to do what she said to be saved, or be physically punished (**Make Cruelty your Best Friend**). And this is when it all went horribly wrong…

[12] Pareidolia is a visual form of Apophenia that I discussed back in Stage 3: Phase 4: Failure with Fallacies on page 96. Have a quick look to remind yourself.

…She said that Armageddon was going to happen in the year 2000!

HOW MANY TIMES DO I HAVE TO SAY THIS?

DON'T GIVE A DATE FOR ARMAGEDDON!

She also made a very specific condition for the way it was going to happen. She foresaw that everyone who wasn't inside her church on the day of reckoning would burn in Hell because of their sinful ways; a very 'cite specific' literal use of '**Demonize the Outside World**', you'd have to agree!

Leading up to the year 2000, Mwerinde told her minions that there was no point in keeping their money or property, and that… yes, you've guessed it, they should give it all to her. As the New Year came and trundled on, minions started to question the veracity of the visions. As the months passed, they started to ask where all their donations had gone! Not a sustainable position to be in as a Cult Leader. Most would have left and tried to start again elsewhere; not Mwerinde! She went on a killing spree that culminated on March the 15th, with the final minions herded into her Church with the promise of salvation, the doors being nailed shut, and the church burnt to the ground taking everyone inside with it. It's estimated that close to a thousand people died, although, all told, it could even be more. It was originally believed to be yet another mass suicide by a 'crazy Cult', but the subsequent investigation revealed the truth. It is thought that Mwerinde escaped to Congo, but she has never been heard from again.

The Lesson is simple, if people believe that the end is nigh, there's a good chance that it will be… for them!

Murder

In the case of Aum Shinrikyo, they tried to kill some judges who were making a decision on a court case of theirs, and they also killed a lawyer and his family because he was investigating their illegal activity. They thought that, by killing them, it would get rid of the problem, but of course, it did the opposite. When Shoko Asahara realized that the police were about to shut his Cult down, he was left with no alternative but to do a rush job on Armageddon! He, along with many of the minions, were arrested and imprisoned.

Then there's the Peoples Temple… yes, Jim Jones was able to arrange both murders and a mass suicide within the same Cult… he really screwed things up!

When a U.S. Congressman flew down to Guyana to investigate concerns that some families had over the conditions of their loved ones (**Disconnection from Loved Ones**), Jim Jones had him and his team killed to avoid any accountability. Jones knew, however, that more people would follow to investigate the disappearance of the Congressman (which begs the question of why he had him killed in the first place?) and that's when, to escape the whole mess, he ordered the mass suicide. Wrong on so many Levels!

The overall Lesson is to not commit murder or order suicide!

The Afterlife

I'm obviously not talking about the spiritual kind of afterlife as we all know that there is no such thing; when you're dead, you're dead. **Let's face it. If someone actually believed that they were going to be judged when they died, they wouldn't behave in such a selfish and abusive manner as Cult Leaders do, would they?**

What I'm really talking about is the afterlife of the Cult when the Cult Leader is no longer around, whether it is because of death, imprisonment or permanent exile, evading the authorities.

Without a strong leader at the helm, a Cult could die out, but what tends to happen is that it splits into different factions, fighting for top billing as the 'One True' version of the faith.

This is what happened to Aum Shinrikyo when Asahara was imprisoned and then executed. One of his daughters thought that it should continue down the family line, changing the name of the Cult to Aleph, whilst one of the high-ranking officials within the Cult is leading an opposing branch (Hikari no Wa). Most minions are just confused about the whole thing, as they rightly should be!

The same sort of thing happened to the Hare Krishna Cult in the late 70's when Swami Prabhupada died in 1977. There was a lot of infighting – with actual murders – between potential leaders. The Cult is still reeling from these conflicts.

Why am I telling you all of this? After all, why should a Cult Leader worry about what happens to his Cult after his death? He's enjoyed his time, used people for his own ends, and clearly doesn't actually care about the future of his minions, correct?

True, but you need to see the bigger picture. If you can't be bothered to go to all the trouble of setting up a Cult, you could always take over an already-existing one.

> *"States that are hereditary and tied to the bloodline of their Prince are easier to maintain than new ones."*
>
> *"The Prince who seizes the opportunity of the rebellion has fewer scruples about securing his position by punishing offenders, flushing out suspects, and strengthening all the places where he is weakest."*
>
> **'The Prince' by Niccolò Machiavelli**

David Koresh knew all about this when he joined the Branch Davidians in 1981 at the tender age of 22. David – known then by his real name, Vernon Howell – went straight to the top by dating the widow of the recently deceased Cult Leader, Ben Roden. Lois Roden was in her late 70's at the time, so the 'bumping of bones' couldn't have been very nice for Vernon but, hey, anything to be in power, right?

Unfortunately for Vernon, a bit like in Aum Shinrikyo, the son of Ben Roden, George, thought that the power should be handed down the bloodline, rather than given to a little 'toy boy'. Sleeping with the Boss's Wife wasn't enough and it ended in an actual shoot-out between the two factions. Luckily for Vernon, George Roden was soon incarcerated into a mental asylum for also killing his roommate with an axe (don't ask!), and that allowed Vernon – reborn as David Koresh – to take over.

A takeover is also what Hon-Ming Chen did with his Cult, Chen Tao. He was already a member of a Cult, run by a woman called Yu-Hsia Chen (no relation!). Originally, he thought that she was the physical representation of God on Earth… until she disagreed with him about where her Cult should be going… then she was nothing to him. He proclaimed that she was a charlatan and that he was the 'One True Leader' (**Embracing Hypocrisy** at its finest!). He hijacked many of her minions over to his new Cult and moved to America. He was successful for a while but the confusion between the similar Cults did weaken his position.

This kind of messy, harmful 'break up' could have happened in Scientology when L Ron Hubbard died from a heart attack in 1986, but David Miscavige had other plans. Taking Machiavelli at his word, it is said that Miscavige seized the opportunity of Hubbard's ill health to carry out a pre-emptive strike on anyone who he saw as a threat, flushing out any potential rivals and expelling them from the Cult, paving the way for himself as the successor.

This is the Lesson for taking over a Cult. The tactic is dependent on absolute ruthlessness. You have to be immensely goal-driven, super-aggressive, and incredibly callous for it to work… you know, the kind of traits that belong to a psychopath! And as we say in the Cult Industry – "*You don't have to be a psychopath to be a Cult Leader... actually you do!*"

Now, don't get me wrong. I am <u>not</u> saying that David Miscavige is a narcissistic, abusive, manipulating psychopath.

I'm not saying it...
… for legal reasons!

Lesson 6: Reflections upon Humanity

One of the biggest obstacles that can trip up a Cult Leader is self-imposed. It is tempting to look at all of the ridiculous lies and offensive behaviour that you are committing, and think that you are going to be found out as a charlatan; that the public will see right through you for what you are – a selfish con artist! Hopefully, your undying narcissism will protect you from such doubts, but if it doesn't, let me put your mind at rest. **You should never give the human race so much credit for being this sensible... they are no way near as rational as they think they are!**

I ask you to remember, and to remind yourself on a regular basis, a couple of hard truths about the reality of being human.

Truth 1: The human brain is heavily flawed!
Some people might already accept this, but even they will over-estimate their brain's capabilities. The thing is, the brain doesn't perceive things as they really are, but rather makes a 'best guess' at the stimuli that it receives, referencing other information and memories as a guide; interpreting the world as it goes along. This process has served us well as a species, allowing humans to flourish where other animals have died out, but it is far from perfect and can let us down in many ways.

For example, the brain can use perspective to gauge the size of an object, but it can get it wrong. Look at the pillars to the right. Which pillar is the biggest? (Clue: They're the same size!) Even after being told that they are the same size, it is difficult to accept it. It's tempting to find an excuse for why they may not be (the artist has made a mistake), instead of using a ruler and just accepting that we got it wrong.

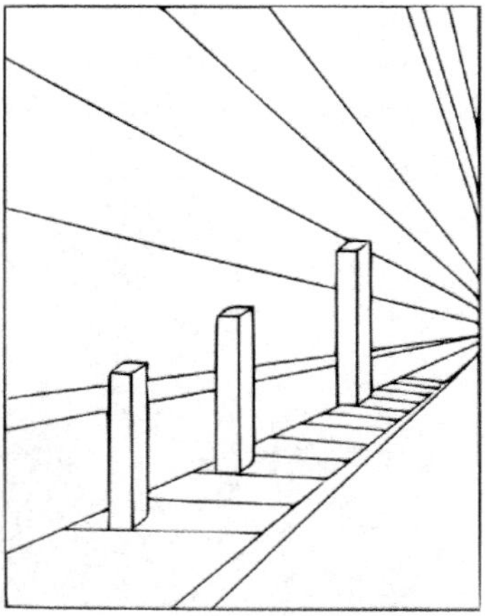

It has been crucial for us as a species to recognize patterns in the world, and understand the connections between phenomena - social cohesion, agricultural and industrial developments, weather and environmental predictions, etc. Generally, we are very good at it… but it isn't perfect, and we can REALLY screw things up, as I have previously mentioned with things like **Apophenia** and **Pareidolia, Creeping Normality** and **Pseudo-Causality**.

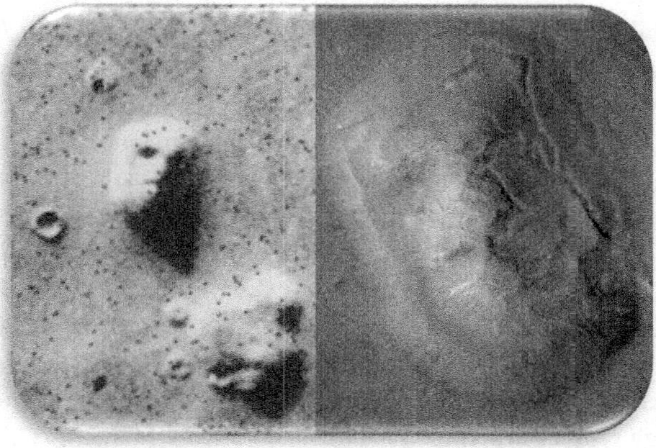

Is this a face on Mars….? Nope, just a rock formation!

Human memory is VERY flawed. The brain is not like the hard-drive of a computer. Humans do not remember things as they really happen, but rather as they WANT to remember them happening. But it's worse than this. More studies are proving that our opinions and previous experiences actually 'colour' our interpretations of the events as they happen (Gestalt Theory), so two or more people at the SAME event, will experience the event differently, not just remember it differently. A double whammy, and the reason why anecdotal accounts are not worth the paper they are written on.

Phenomena like the **Placebo** and **Nocebo Effects**, along with the developing **Epigenetic** research, prove that the external environment can directly manipulate both the neurological and physiological processes of a human being. The human brain is far from being a perfect organ!

Truth 2: Humans have flawed cognitive processes.
Ok, most people won't be surprised at this one, particularly if they've ever spoken to someone who thinks that the world is flat, but those same people will still not see how bad things really are.

When making decisions, humans rarely carefully consider all of the evidence before rationally coming to a calculated conclusion. Studies have shown that humans tend to make choices based upon emotional appeals and 'gut reactions', and only then do they rationalize those choices afterwards (*Iowa Gambling Task – Bechara, Damasio et al*). Humans are able to use tremendous acts of **Cognitive Dissonance** to delude themselves into thinking that they DID make logical decisions, even when this is blatantly false. Humans are far more influenced by their biased perceptions and by any information that supports their values and opinions, than facts or evidence to the contrary (**Confirmation Bias**). Along with many other flaws such as **Circular Logic**, the **Barnum Effect**, **Herd Mentality**, **False Dichotomies**, and **Target Blindness**, it's, quite frankly, a wonder that the human race still exists!

Interestingly, most of these flaws could largely be negated through regular practice of Mindful Awareness, Critical Thinking, Pluralism and Skepticism. If every child was taught about these subjects throughout their education, they would be given the tools to deal with the kind of flawed processes that they could be subjected to in their everyday lives. Luckily for Cult Leaders, it would be a conflict of interest for any government to introduce such subjects into the National Curriculum. After all, would politicians want the public to learn how to recognize false claims and flawed arguments? It could make their jobs a nightmare!

So, the Lesson is simple. Humans are a very easy mark!
The idea of 'Free Will' is a misnomer, as humans are 'chained' directly to memories and experiences; as much influenced by external factors as internal ones, and you can take advantage of this by being that 'external factor'. But don't let your minions know about it. Deceive them by saying that they really do have independent freewill and absolute autonomy. That way, you'll be able to fully control and manipulate them AND they will convince themselves that it was their 'choice' to become a slave. Brilliant!

Checklist for Stage 5

I think you'll agree that the extra Lessons were worth it. It's not enough to work through my **6** Steps to creating a perfect Cult Leader persona, and to construct a seductive Cult using my **6**-Part template. It's only half the story to gently lead someone through the **6** Phases of Metamorphosis, and to pile on the **6** Levels of oppression afterwards.

To fully appreciate how a Cult works and how a Cult Leader can be so successful, **you need to consider ALL of the factors that lead to their absolute control and devotion.**

You need to understand why placing yourself as a victim can really enforce conformity within your Cult, and can allow you to dodge any valid criticisms or accountability for your actions.

You need to understand how language and imagery can help with manipulating your minions and deflecting any media scrutiny. A simple sidestep into the 'Blackhole' of debate that is Semantics, by getting wrapped up in the definitions of 'Cults' and 'Religions' for example, can create such a smokescreen that you'll be able to creep away unnoticed from any awkward questions or investigations. After all, it doesn't matter what your group is called; what you don't want people to focus on is your abusive behavior towards your minions. **Semantics can get you out of a very sticky corner**!

Hopefully, you'll already understand that it is wrong to kill, whether it's your minions or someone from the Outside World, but it's vital that you understand that it's possible to tackle the meddling authorities… without resorting to mass murder.

Finally, I hope you understand how flawed humans really are, and how, without them learning the skill sets to counter your techniques of control, they are sitting ducks for your desires.

If you can do all of this, dear reader, then you will know what it takes to become a great Cult Leader. And you will deserve the wonderful Special Bonus that awaits. By the way, the next Stage was going to be in the book anyway (it needed to be in there to make the Stages up to **6**!), but using phrases like '**Special Bonus**' can really trigger the **Jackpot Mentality** in people. Good Luck.

Answer the following questions… well, you know the drill!

<u>End of Stage 5 Quiz</u>

Answer the questions below and see how you have scored.

Question 1) When should you apply the Persecution Principle?

A) Whenever I want to avoid valid criticisms of my lies and abusive behaviour… so, all of the time!

B) Whenever I want to use fear to unify my minions into conformity… so, all of the time!

C) Never. Pretending to be persecuted devalues the suffering of genuine victims of persecution.

Question 2) Which words would you use when dealing with the media?

A) "*The aura created by the energy from our spiritual essences can guide us, like a lighthouse in the fog of ignorance.*"

B) I wouldn't 'deal' with the evil Outside World. It's doomed!

C) Honest ones that fairly represent my thoughts and values.

Question 3) How would you avoid interference from Outside Authorities?

A) I would 'invest' some financial support into local groups and organizations.

B) I would harass them until they back off!

C) I wouldn't avoid them. There should always be independent accountability as part of a fair and progressive process.

Question 4) How are children beneficial to a Cult?

A) It is easy to make, manipulate and mold them.

B) Minions can be controlled by the threat of losing a child.

C) Children should not be used as instruments of control.

Question 5) Why shouldn't you kill someone who is interfering with your Cult?

A) Because it triggers greater interference.

B) EXACTLY! Why shouldn't I?

C) Because it is unethical and illegal.

Question 6) What flaws in Human behaviour can be best utilized by a Cult?

A) My favorite is **Cognitive Dissonance** as it tends to make the minions do the work in controlling themselves for me.

B) All of them… and there are loads! HA! HA! HA!

C) We should help each other to overcome our flaws by using a good understanding of Critical Thinking, Pluralism, Skepticism and Mindful Awareness.

How did you do?

Mostly A's – You have reached perfection! You deserve the Special Bonus! Enjoy your bright new Golden future!

Mostly B's – You've done OK. You're an OK Cult Leader! OK?

Mostly C's – You're an insult to Cult Leaders everywhere! I hope that they take you outside and teach you a Lesson of their own!

Stage Six:

‘Special Bonus’ Section

Best of the Best

Example 1: Happy Science (Kofuku no Kagaku)

Cult Leader: Ryuho Okawa (real name is Takashi Nakagawa before his Transformational Epiphany).

Cult Details: Created in Japan in 198**6**.
Aim: Money and Adulation.
Theme: Asian Fusion with a soupçon of Pseudo-Science and Science Fiction – (Okawa really threw everything into the mix!)
Structure: Open Societal, with Closed 'Training Retreats' for the Indoctrination process (**IsoDep**).

Cult Leader Details: Born in 195**6** in Shikoku, Japan, he trained to be a financial trader. His life seemed to be set as a Japanese 'Salary Man' until, in 1981, whilst he was working for his company

in New York, he was contacted by the spirit dimension and was 'awakened' to the news that, instead of being a boring trader in a large corporation, he was, in fact, 'Lord El Cantare', the Supreme God of the Earth! His universal purpose was to save the people of Earth from destruction. Having received this life-changing news…
he waited five years before he resigned and started his Cult in 198**6** - (as I've said before, – "*Take a few years off and prepare yourself; cults aren't built overnight, you know.*" – Stage 1: Step 1, Page 19)

As 'The Grand Saviour' - (**False Title of Importance**), Okawa is able to channel all the many truths directly from the essence of El Cantare into numerous books and seminar workshops, that can then bring salvation to the people of Earth… at a price, of course!

With great sacrifice to his own personal life, he was willing to become a multi-millionaire, adored by thousands of minions, and has tirelessly tried to save humans from failure! He isn't alone in this task. Luckily, Okawa married Kyoko Kimura, who just so happened to be the reincarnation of the Greek Goddess, Aphrodite - (now, that's a **Supporting Witness** worth having!) Unluckily, she started to publicly point out his corrupt behaviour and they divorced in 2011. Luckily, he then married Shio Kondo, who just so happened to be the reincarnation of the Greek Goddess, Gaia - (he obviously has a thing for Greek women!) We'll see how long this Goddess lasts.

Cult Mythology: Lord El Cantare is the head of a spirit group in charge of Earth, and answers to the Creator of our Universe. This group resides in the Ninth Dimension of the Spirit World, of which there are over 20 dimensions, and their task is to guide their creations (humans) towards salvation before the Earth is destroyed.

Their wondrous knowledge stems from the fact that this isn't the first time that they've developed a Utopian world. El Cantare, who's original name was El Miore, was the ruler of Venus about **6** billion years ago, and he created a Venusian species, much like humans, but with IQ's over 300! This species evolved to find perfect harmony, and travelled through the Universe on spaceships.

Unfortunately, El Miore got a message from the Creator of the Universe (Fundamental God), that He had planned to set off a massive volcano on Venus that would destroy life on the planet… (a bit inconsiderate of Him) and that El Miore needed to start again.

So, El Miore changed his name to El Cantare… for some reason, and took some of his Venusian beings and fused them with other Cosmic species with pointy ears and long tails to create humans. He split them into two groups. One group, he gave wisdom and courage; the other group, he gave elegance and grace… (I think we can see where this is going!) This, according to Okawa, is how men and women came to be… (Yep, he went there!).

Since then, El Cantare, in many different forms, like Jesus, the Buddha, and now Okawa, has been trying to educate humans so that they can reach perfect harmony… hopefully before the Creator of our Universe sets off another massive bloody volcano![13]

Rating: 6/6. According to its website, Happy Science is now the biggest religion in Japan (so much for Shinto and Buddhism then!) and has spread across the globe, with 12 million members in over 140 countries (no citation has been given for any of these 'stats'!)

Mr. Okawa is a multi-millionaire, with adoring minions where ever he goes. He is able to do all of this with very little scrutiny from the media or authorities, seemingly staying under the radar. It is, therefore, one of the most successful Cults around. Brilliant!

OK. It's a bit boring to use his initials as the Cult's symbol, but at least it does re-enforce his authority.

[13] This is taken from the first chapter of 'The Laws of the Sun'; one of over 2,600 publications Okawa has made! Remember, lots of books means lots of money!

Example 2: Aetherius Society

Cult Leader: Dr King, although his full title has been stated as 'His Eminence Sir George King, O.S.P, Ph.D., Th. D, D.D., Metropolitan Archbishop of the Aetherius Churches'… but I think that this is taking the **False Title of Importance** a bit too far… even for a Cult Leader! His real name was just George King before his Transformational Epiphany.

Cult Details: Created in the United Kingdom in 1955.
Aim: Adulation (with enough money for a good living).
Theme: Science Fiction (with a good dollop of Asian Fusion).
Structure: Open Societal, with Closed 'Mountain Pilgrimages' for the Indoctrination process **(IsoDep)**.

Cult Leader Details: Born in 1919, King was brought up in a deeply Christian family but spent his formative years exploring other religious beliefs. In the 1940's, after he had moved to London to be a taxi driver, he took up yoga and was so good at it,

he developed psychic powers! One morning in 1954, when he was washing the dishes in his small flat in Maida Vale, West London, he was contacted by the Master Aetherius, a superior Being from Venus. The voice in the room told him – "*Prepare yourself! You are to become the voice of Interplanetary Parliament.*" George was unsure if this had really happened, but then, a few days later, when he was visited by a world-renowned Yoga teacher, who was in India at the same time, but had used an advanced yogic technique to travel to London, enter through a locked door without opening it, speak to him, and then go back to India, all in the same day, George was convinced of the truth that he had been given.

Once it was explained to George that he was to be The Primary Terrestrial Mental Channel (a better **False Title of Importance**), he set up The Aetherius Society in 1955. He then dedicated himself to saving Mother Earth, raising the consciousness of humanity in unique and powerful ways, and saving humans from themselves.

He travelled the world, passing on the teachings from the aliens in numerous books that he 'translated', until he died in California in 1997. Not bad for a taxi driver from London!

Cult Mythology: Mother Earth is a living Goddess who has sacrificed her own evolution to provide a home for humankind – a backward and often barbaric race. There are many advanced extraterrestrial civilizations on other planets in this solar system, but science cannot detect them because they exist at higher plains or 'frequencies of vibration' on those planets (as I mentioned on page **62** – "*Always make them invisible as this will prevent anyone from proving you wrong!*") These Beings, like Master Aetherius from Venus, have often visited Earth, in order to help humans become a more advanced species. They have been called Jesus, Buddha, Sri Krishna, Confucius and Lao Tzu, but they are known to the minions as 'Cosmic Masters'.

If humans can properly learn the wisdom of these Cosmic Masters, by buying and reading all of Dr Kings teachings, they will fulfill their full potential. Luckily, humans have time to do this, as they go through many incarnations before reaching enlightenment (Yes, there is karmic reincarnation in there as well!). When, after many lives, humans have properly learnt all the lessons, they are allowed to leave the 'Wheel of Rebirth' and start a higher experience cycle on another planet, becoming a Cosmic Master themselves.

Now, you might be thinking to yourself – "*Hang on, this all sounds very familiar, what with aliens from Venus, and Jesus and Buddha being extraterrestrial, and aliens communicating to us through the Cult Leader, etc.*", but you must remember my advice from Stage 2: Part 5: Motivational Mythology on page **66** – "*Always appropriate the familiar. Don't create, just incorporate.*"

Rating: 6/6. This one is a reminder that not all successful Cults need to be large international conglomerates. If the aim of the Cult Leader is to be admired by every person who follows him, and to live a good life, then George's Cult was a great success. Yes, he was a pale imitation of L Ron Hubbard (who created a similar Cult at the same time), but you know what… the taxi driver did good! Besides, since his death in 1997, the Cult has been drifting. Perhaps it needs a vibrant, young Cult Leader to take it over… nudge, nudge, wink, wink!

George King joined a stylized symbol of Hinduism with a pyramid… that represents knowledge… apparently!

Example 3: Raëlism

Cult Leader: Prophet or Maitreya Raël (real name is Claude Maurice Marcel Vorilhon before his Transformational Epiphany).

Cult Details: Created in France in 1973.
Aim: Sex (with a bit of money thrown in).
Theme: Science Fiction (with a bit of Asian Fusion thrown in).
Structure: Open Societal, with Tantric Sex Retreats for the Indoctrination process (**IsoDep**). Works for me!

Cult Leader Details: Born in 1946 to a Jewish father and an Atheist mother, he ran away to Paris when he was a teenager and tried to make it as a musician. When that failed to go anywhere, he started writing as a sports journalist and later created his own Sports Car magazine. Then, in 1973, whilst he was riding his bike in the hills of a volcanic park, a UFO landed and an alien got out called Yahweh. They chatted for a while and Yahweh explained to Claude that he had been chosen to bring all of the knowledge that the aliens, called Elohim, wanted to give to the people of Earth (you know, just like many other Cult Leaders have done!)

Claude quit his job, changed his name to Maitreya Raël, and set up his Cult. Since then, he has written many books that 'translate' what the aliens have told him. He travels the world, trying to spread love and happiness to the peoples of the planet. He has been married three times, and been divorced three times. Apparently, the wives don't like it when he spreads the love too much!

Cult Mythology: The Elohim are an advanced extraterrestrial species that used Earth as an experimental playground. Using their advanced genetic technology, they created all life on the planet, including humans, which they created in their own image. Since then, they have been visiting the planet in various guises, like… (yep, you guessed it), Jesus, the Buddha, Confucius, …and the rest! Over the millennia, the teachings from such figures have been twisted and tarnished with false readings. If humans can learn the 'proper truth', by following the teachings of Maitreya Raël, they will be taken up into space when the aliens return.

Rating: 5/**6**. Many people have spotted the obvious 'cut and pasting' that Claude has used for his 'writings', with Claude losing many libel cases over the years; and he does cut a very sad figure, as he tries to spread the love with young women, having now become bald, old and wrinkly! But you know what, he still has thousands of followers and he lives a pretty good lifestyle for such an old codger. Good on him!

The symbol used for Raëlism!

Can you see how Claude fused the Jewish Star of David with the Hindu swastika? Cheeky!

Always appropriate the familiar!

Example 4: Church of Bible Understanding - COBU

Cult Leader: Stewart Tanner Traill (He is one of the few Cult Leaders who didn't change his name; although he did become known by one of his ex-minions as - Stewart 'I made off with the money and the woman and left you with nothing of value' Traill… but I don't think that this was ever an official title!)

Cult Details: Created in USA in 1977.
Aim: Money and Sex (the perfect combo!).
Theme: Religion.
Structure: Closed Society with some of the properties (called Training Centres) used for the Indoctrination process (**IsoDep**).

Cult Leader Details: Born in 1936 in Quebec, Canada, Stewart's father, who was a Presbyterian Preacher, then took his family to Allentown, Pennsylvania. Stewart rejected Christianity as a teenager, and left university after only a few semesters, citing that he was more intelligent than Albert Einstein and had a brighter future than formal education could provide. He then married a 16-year-old girl and became a vacuum repairman.

By the mid-1960's, having been married for over 10 years and having 5 children, he suddenly had the revelation that Jesus wanted him to go out into the world and spread the 'true' word of the Bible (At least he didn't think that he WAS Jesus, I suppose!) He started to build a network of followers, stealing them from other groups, and then set up a Cult called Forever Family (FF) in 1971. Talking of stealing, Stewart 'appropriated' ideas from other preachers and writers to create a figure system and colour code for understanding the Bible, which he then taught as his own… like any good Cult Leader should! He forced his minions to use 'strong arm' sales tactics to get new minions and buy new centres, and used those minions as free labour for his various businesses, which grew from strength to strength. So much so, that he was able to buy his own planes to spread the truth, and he would take young female minions on his flying trips to 'give him a hand', if you know what I mean?

By 1976, his wife was sick and tired of his 'joy rides' and openly exposed his corrupt behaviour within the Cult. Along with other abuse charges by other minions, Stewart knew that he had to do something. So, he divorced her, and started afresh by creating a new Cult called the Church of Bible Understanding (COBU) in 1977. Now in his 40's, he married a young minion of 19 years and continued with spreading the true word of the Bible, even opening new centres world-wide. Some of the old minions left and new minions came along. Problem solved!

By the mid-80's, however, his second wife started to wise up and complained about his abusive adulterous behaviour. This is when he made a fundamental mistake. He admitted to being wrong... NEVER ADMIT TO BEING WRONG! He apologized for his behaviour and promised to change. What was he thinking? Many of his minions lost faith in him and left. He struggled for many years to get things back on track. He obviously carried on playing around with other women and his wife started to complain again. Just as it was looking like he would have to start yet another Cult, he accidently crashed his car on the passenger side, whilst his wife was sitting there, and she ended up in hospital, severely debilitated. Stewart didn't accept that it was his fault and claimed that, as she now couldn't fulfil her wedding vows, he was no longer married to her in the eyes of God. He shacked up with a daughter of one of his minions, who was more than 40 years younger than him. His businesses kept bringing in the money and he continued to spread the true word of the Bible until he died in 2018.

Cult Mythology: The Master has a true understanding of the Bible, and if you commit to The Master... by doing whatever he says, donating 90% of your wages to him, or volunteering for his successful multi-million-dollar businesses, you will find salvation.

Rating: 5/6. It was touch and go a few times but he got away with it. He lived a millionaire lifestyle with young women at his beck and call, large mansions in beautiful places; planes, cars and all the bling. Unbelievable, right?

Example 5: Unification Church (Moonies)

Cult Leader: Sun Myung Moon (real name was Mun Yong-Myeong before his Transformational Epiphany).

Cult Details: Created in Seoul, South Korea in 1954.
Aim: Money, Power and Adulation.
Theme: Religion (a 'quirky' take on Christianity!)
Structure: Open Societal, with Closed 'Training Retreats' for the Indoctrination process (**IsoDep**).

Cult Leader Details: Born in 1920 in what is now North Korea, Moon lived a very simple farming life. When he was 10 years old, his family converted from Confucianism to Christianity, joining the Presbyterian Church. When he was 15, Jesus came to him and told him that he was to finish the work that Jesus had started. So, **6** years later, he went to Japan and studied Electrical Engineering! During this time, he was contacted by Abraham, Moses, Jesus, the Buddha and other sages, who gave him enough knowledge that he could write his own book called the 'Divine Principles'; a sequel to the Bible. He then married his first wife, Sun Kil Choi in 1945.

A couple of years later, Moon was told by God to leave his wife and new-born son and preach the word in North Korea, where he was promptly convicted of spying and sent to a prison camp for 5 years. He escaped in 1950 and fled to South Korea.

Throughout this tumultuous time, he had been developing his religious beliefs and, in 1954, he formally founded the 'Holy Spirit Association for the Unification of World Christianity'; thankfully shortened to the Unification Church. He was now able to bring a true understanding of Christianity to the world using his 'Divine Principles', with values based upon a Conservative, Family-orientated system. He then divorced his wife in 1957, having had another child by a different woman (**Embrace Hypocrisy!**)

His Cult became very successful and he tied it in with many businesses that he set up... not to cash in on the success, you understand. He remarried in 1960 to Hak Ja Han and only slipped up one more time by having another child with a different woman in 1966... that we know of!

In 1971, God told Moon to move his whole family to America and bring the true understanding of Christianity to that nation… which I'm sure went down well! Moon continued to set up more successful billion-dollar businesses whilst in the USA. In 1982, however, he was charged with tax fraud and went to prison again. Upon his release, he carried on spreading the true understanding of Christianity by living an opulent life, arranging mass weddings, and rubbing shoulders with presidents and dictators alike. He continued to do the work that Jesus had started, bringing peace to the World, until he died from pneumonia and organ failure in 2012.

Cult Mythology: Adam and Eve were supposed to bring peace and harmony to mankind (that was yet to exist!), but because Eve really screwed it up with the snake/apple thing, the chance was lost. Jesus was also meant to do the same with Mary Magdalene, but before he had a chance to get married, Jesus was abruptly stopped … by a cross. Now, it is third time lucky with Moon and Han (presumably we're to ignore the other women, of course!), and if humans can follow the teachings of their 'True Parents', there will be unified peace on Earth. Apparently, the fact that Moon died some time ago, has no bearings on the matter whatsoever!

Rating: 6/6. A multi-billion-dollar organization. A wealthy, exorbitant life-style with fast cars and large mansions. Devoted minions across the world. Let's face it… What didn't he do right? Even with several imprisonments, illegitimate children, divorces, and other corruption allegations, Sun Myung Moon and his family are still seen as divine Beings by their minions. Top Marks!!

Example 6: Scientology

Cult Leader: L Ron Hubbard (real name is Lafayette Ronald Hubbard before his Transformational Epiphany… although, for a fantasy writer, you'd think he could have done better than 'L Ron')

Cult Details: Created in USA, circa 1953.
Aim: Money and Adulation.
Theme: Science Fiction (using Pseudo-Science and Religion as a smoke-screen… and tax benefits!)
Structure: Open Societal, with Compound 'Training Centres' called Orgs for the Indoctrination process (**IsoDep**).

Cult Leader Details: Hubbard was an author, philosopher, humanitarian and Founder of the Scientology religion. He was born March 12, 1911, in Tilden, Nebraska. His long and adventurous road to discovery began at an early age, and was soon reading well beyond his years: Shakespeare, Greek philosophy and an array of later classics. Yet his early years were far from bookish, and with his family's move to Helena, Montana, he was soon breaking broncos with the best of the local wranglers.

As an inquisitive youth in what was then still a rough and tumble American West, he was also soon befriending indigenous Blackfoot Indians – learning tribal lore and legend from a local medicine man, achieving that very rare status of 'blood brother'.

When his father was assigned to the South Pacific as a US naval commander, Ron embarked upon the first of his famed Asian travels. By the age of 19 he had traveled more than a quarter of a million miles and traversed much of China and India. He became one of the few Western adventurers to study with the last in the line of royal magicians from the court of Kublai Khan.

To round out his university days, he also became one of the foremost pioneers of American aviation and a barnstorming sensation across the Midwest. Ultimately, however, and particularly in light of what passed for a 'science of the mind' in university psychology labs, he could only conclude that Western academia held no answers.

By the mid-1930s he was among the most widely read authors in the fabled heyday of American pulp fiction. But he never lost sight of his primary quest. He would eventually study 21 races and cultures while searching out an underlying 'common denominator of existence' upon which to build a workable philosophy for the betterment of Man.

With the advent of the Second World War, Ron entered the United States Navy as a lieutenant. He went on to serve with distinction on both the North Pacific and Atlantic. Left partially blind and lame from his injuries sustained in combat, he fully regained his own health by practicing the procedures he had developed for alleviating trauma, known as Dianetics.

By pursuing 'further research into life force', he soon realized that this life force was intrinsically spiritual and extended well beyond any one lifetime. This realization led to the creation of Scientology. Ron continues his research in the Universe, having left his mortal body in 198**6**[14].

Cult Mythology: An alien called Xenu was the ruler of a Galactic Confederacy 75 million years ago, consisting of 7**6** planets including Earth. Xenu was about to be deposed, so he gathered billions of the aliens who were against him, froze them, took them to Earth and dropped them near a volcano. He then launched massive hydrogen bombs into the volcano and killed nearly all of them. Millions of years later, the invisible souls of those victims, called Thetans (**Always make them invisible!**), fly around and attach themselves onto humans, negatively effecting the human's ability to find peace and harmony. By learning the teachings of The Master, a person can free themselves of these aliens and develop super powers… at a cost, of course!

Rating: 6/6. Ron lived a millionaire lifestyle, worshipped by millions, and dodged any criminal charges by throwing his minions 'under the bus', including his own wife. He really is the Master of Masters. It's just a shame that Miscavige is royally screwing it up.

---

[14] Extracts lifted directly from Scientologynews.org. Aren't fantasy stories fun? (Correct at time of print).

GLOSSARY

Here are some words and phrases that can help you to understand how people can be controlled. Learn what they are and how they can be used.

Anecdotal Accounts (Page 24). Personal testimony of events or claims that can be fake or, at best, unreliable. The kicker is, however, that humans have traditionally learnt about life from a narrative process; fables, myths, fairy tales, allegories and parables – particularly in childhood, so they are primed to take anecdotal accounts as fact. Very advantageous for a Cult Leader.

Apophenia (Page 96). The neurological phenomena of finding meaningful patterns or connections within trivial or random events. This is usually accompanied by people shouting, "*It's a sign!*"

Barnum Effect (Page 31). Formally known as **The Forer Effect**, it is when a vague or ambiguous statement is seen as meaningful to a specific individual, even though the statement could apply to many people – "*We've got something for everyone!*" - PT Barnum. Horoscopes are based on this effect. It is usually accompanied by the person saying, "*That is so me! How could he know?*"

Binary Landscape (Page 70). The **False** or **Forced Dichotomy** of 'All or Nothing'. This narrow view of the world ignores the multifaceted spectrum of life. The less practice a minion gets of understanding the nuances and complexities of life, the easier it is to manipulate them; they are either with you or against you!

Circular Logic (Page 14). Claims that try to support themselves without any warrants or evidence. Think of a multi-plug extension that's plugged into itself. It's a claim that is easy to make but has no power to it! For example, "*We know our Master is honest because he said he is honest!*"

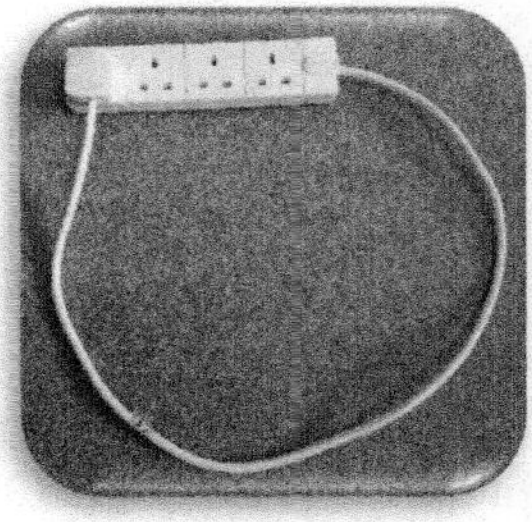

Cocktail Party Effect (Page 96). A neurological process that 'filters out' much of the stimuli that the brain receives in order to operate efficiently in a crowded environment. This selective attention allows the individual to give greater importance to certain stimulus. This filtering system can be recalibrated to include your claims and priorities. (Also see **Confirmation Bias** on Page 22)

Cold Reading (Page 30). A set of techniques that obtain personal information on a stranger using human cues such as body language, reactions to generic phrases, and individual expressions, such as fashion. It is mostly used by psychics and fortune tellers, but Cult Leaders can also use it in the same way.

Cognitive Dissonance (Page 28). The ability to hold two or more opposing ideas or beliefs at the same time. For example, "*Our Master loves us and wants to show us how to live a good life, which is why it is good that he abuses us, in order for us to learn.*"

Confirmation Bias (Page 22). More commonly known as **Cherry Picking**, it is the practice of only observing or remembering information or events that support the person's worldview.

Creeping Normality (Page 80). A slow process of acclimation to a changed reality, usually unnoticed by the individual concerned. Think of a Hoarder, living in ever-increasing squalor. The same can happen to a minion, as they get drawn into the Cult.

Demonizing the Outside World (Page 92). The act of making anything or anyone (especially family, friends and ex-minions) outside of the Cult appear to be evil, poisonous and doomed. This is vitally imperative for a Cult to operate, in order to enforce conformity and oppression of the minions. (Please, please, please read page **92**!)

Destroying the Self (Page 99). The act of breaking down a person's sense of autonomy and individuality, so that they become 'as one' with the Cult; seen as just a cog in the Wheel of Fortune… for the Cult Leader, that is!

Dunning-Kruger Effect (Page 23). It is when a person has such a low ability at a certain task or skillset, that they tend to over-estimate such ability in order to deny this deficiency, yet have such a reduced understanding that they can't even recognise their flaws. The psychologists David Dunning and Justin Kruger state that - "*the miscalibration of the incompetent stems from an error about the Self.*" Just look at the 'Flat-Earth Movement' to get an idea.

Duplicating Insular Systems of Communication (Page 124). More commonly known as **Social Echo Chambers**, these are self-affirming communicational structures that validate and re-enforce claims that are passed between minions, whilst creating suspicion of other contrary messages. This also enforces conformity as minions will not want to go against 'the accepted truth', fearful of being rejected by their peers.

Front Groups (Page 84). Any business or organization that serves as the public face of the Cult, providing a legitimate and seemingly harmless access to potential minions. It normally also serves as an extra revenue stream for the Cult.

Groupthink (Page 88). A psychological phenomenon that is driven by the desire for harmony and conformity; not wishing to 'rock the boat' and be singled out as a trouble maker. This desire can lead to the group as a whole making irrational decisions and committing to submission 'at all cost'. Perfect for a Cult Leader!

Halo Effect (Page 91). A form of **Confirmation Bias** that is based upon a single experience or characteristic of a person or group, that is then forever attributed to that person or group, regardless of how false that opinion turns out to be. It's like putting on Rose-Tinted glasses whenever viewing that person or group.

Herd Mentality (Page 89). A social phenomenon that makes an individual think or act differently than if they were on their own. It is an acute form of peer pressure that allows an individual to feel that they are behaving correctly just because the rest of the group is doing the same. (Also see **Groupthink** on page 88)

Indoctrination (Page 81). A process of learning that demands, usually through a threat of punishment, a lack of critical thinking and examination; fear is an integral part of the indoctrination process, as is repetition. The other factor is repetition. Repetition is really important when it comes to indoctrination… Repetition!

Jackpot Mentality (Page 30). The desire to 'beat the odds' and win big, blinding the person from the irrational decisions that they are making. (Also see **Target Blindness** on Page 98)

Love Bombing (Page 88). The process of smothering a new member with affection and kindness, lulling them into a false sense of security, then placing conditions on that affection to enforce conformity. It is formally known as **Operant Conditioning**.

Minion. A victim of control and manipulation, usually targeted at a time of vulnerability; similar to a Battered Spouse. Although the minion will feel that they are important to the Cult Leader, they will mean nothing to him; just a stepping stone to his happiness… similar to a Battered Spouse.

Nocebo Effect (Page 101). The ability to induce adverse mental and physiological affects just by suggestion alone. It is the 'evil twin' of the Placebo Effect, and can be used both as a form of control and of punishment. When 'cured' by the Placebo Effect, it can also be used as proof of a Cult Leader's powers of healing.

Pareidolia (Page 97). The phenomenon of discerning something definite and clear within a formless, nondescript image or sound. It is a visual or audio version of **Apophenia** on page 96. Good examples of these would be seeing the face of Jesus on a slice of toast or hearing the voice of a dead person in the static of an untuned radio.

The Persecution Principle (Page 137). The action of feigning victimization in order to avoid criticism, and/or to enforce group cohesion, and/or to receive unjust privilege.

Placebo Effect (Page 101). The ability to induce beneficial mental and physiological affects just by suggestion alone. A treatment using a Placebo will have no direct causal ingredient, but the subject will believe that it does, in some way, from the authority that administers it. That's where a Cult Leader can come in.

Pseudo Causality (Page 95). A fabricated link between 2 or more unconnected events. A form of Non Sequitur called '*cum* or *post hoc ergo propter hoc*' (Latin for *with* or *after this*, *therefore because of this*).

The Psychology of Previous Investment (Page 130). Formally known as the **Sunk Cost Fallacy**, it is a process of denial, by which the collective commitments to a decision makes it increasingly difficult to reassess or change that decision, as doing so would lead the individual to admit that their choices had been a mistake.

Reluctant Narrative (Page 39). A feigned position of humble hesitance, where the Cult Leader 'regrettably' takes on the position of authority, not because he wants to, but because his high sense of moral responsibility MAKES him do so. Honest… wink, wink!

Target Blindness (Page 98). The natural sense of achievement that is gained by 'reaching a goal' can be used against a minion, by setting arbitrary targets and challenges and watching them 'chase their tails', blind to how much control they have lost.

Thought-Stopping Rituals (Page 97). Meditation, chanting, dancing, or any other repetitive activity which switches off the analytical part of the brain. Most of these physical activities can increase the levels of serotonin, dopamine and endorphins that leave the individual feeling blissfully relaxed, which can then be framed as a 'spiritual experience'.

Transformational Epiphany (Page 14). A fabricated experience that confers wisdom, power, and respect onto the 'received' person. It allows the person's 'dodgy' past to be wiped clean, and its transformational quality elevates that person to a special status.

The One Real Truth

A Genuine Personal Message From the Real Authors

If you have got to this page by reading the whole book, we doff our caps to you… it is a rough ride through a very dark and scary landscape!

If you have got to this page by jumping straight to it, we don't blame you… it is a rough ride through a very dark and scary landscape!

What is the aim of this book?
Imagine that you are standing outside a large theatre, with a long queue of people who are waiting to go and see a mystical magician. On a large banner, it reads – "*The Mighty Majestic Marvolio can create genuine magic before your very eyes! Tickets just £600!*"

Now, it's one thing to enjoy an entertaining magic show done by incredible artists like Penn & Teller or Derren Brown, but it's another thing for people to be suckered into believing something that isn't true, particularly when it could lead to suffering and harm. If you knew that someone was going to be harmed by such trickery, wouldn't you tell them how the tricks are done, so that they wouldn't be fooled[15]? THAT is the aim of this book.

What is a cult?
The first mistake that most people make when it comes to identifying a cult is to try and create a precise and comprehensive definition of one. This is a 'red herring', as most social constructs have blurred edges to them, with parallel practices and similar concepts. Many educational systems, for example, use repetition for learning (**page 82**), and both the armed forces and some therapy methods work at breaking down the Self (**page 99**).

No, the best thing to do is to not worry about neat pigeon-holes or hard-edged boxes, and focus on the harmful traits, features and

[15] Would a 'genuine' magician need to use such trickery?

practices that are found in most cults; factors which lead to such terrible suffering for both the individual and the families involved.

But it's not just cults where this kind of abuse and manipulation occurs. This book also uses cults as a lens to focus on such practices found in other walks of life, such as consumerism, politics, social media, and even personal relationships. The lessons learnt from this book can be applied to every aspect of our lives. **This is the only book you will ever need to read to find absolute perfection and never-ending happiness...**

...THAT is a complete lie; read as many books as possible! But this is the kind of emotive, absolutist language that you'll need to look out for when dealing with such manipulative systems. OK?

How can I know if I have joined a cult?

You can't. Sorry. Cults annoyingly won't call themselves cults, and it is rarely obvious that a group is, in fact, a cult – by design. Apart from reading this book several times to familiarize yourself with their techniques and traits, the key to the problem is to see it 'in the whole' and become wary only when the majority of the characteristics are found in the group that you've just joined. It is when these traits, features and practices are taken '**as a collective, cumulative picture**' that you should have cause for concern.

Here are some questions that you should ask yourself, and if you answer 'Yes' to MOST of them, then be afraid... be very afraid! Also, ask yourself these questions every 3 months to see if anything changes within you over time (read **page 80** to understand why).

1) Has the leader of the group had some kind of experience or epiphany that radically changed his view of the world? (Please see **page 14** for more details)

2) Is the leader certain about their position and will not entertain other possible viewpoints? (Please see **page 20**)

3) Does the leader live a different lifestyle to the other members? Has he a privileged life because of his position? (See **page 26**)

4) Is the leader the only person who really understands the truth? (Please see **page 30**)

5) Does the leader pretend to be humble but, underneath it all, is very arrogant? Be honest now! (Please see **page 37**)

6) Is the leader aggressive or cruel to some members of the group; perhaps phrasing it as a necessary act of being 'cruel to be kind'? (Please see **page 41**)

7) Does the group think that people outside of the group are evil and doomed to failure? (Please see **page 92**)

8) Does the group have a very simplistic 'black or white' view of the world, ignoring complexity and nuance? (See **page 70**)

9) Does the group discourage or even ban contact with ex-members or family from outside the group? (See **page 120**)

10) Does the group talk about some type of apocalypse, whether it is for the whole world or in terms of a personal disaster? (Please see **page 53**)

11) Does the group regularly claim that they are being victimized by outside forces? (Please see **page 137**)

12) Does the group make newcomers feel loved, but then withhold that love if they don't 'toe the line'? Be honest now! (Please see **page 88**)

13) Does the group discourage or prevent members from reading alternative opinions and viewpoints? (See **page 124**)

How did you do? Were most of them 'Yes'? Then be aware that you could be in an abusive, controlling group. **Awareness is half the battle.** It might be an idea to leave!

How do I get a Loved One out of a cult?

You can't. Sorry. Cults are the worst form of addiction, as BOTH the addict and the 'addiction' are actively conspiring to keep the addiction going. It used to be a common practice to try and physically remove members from a cult without their consent, but that can create more harm than good, both for the Loved One and the family involved, as the Loved One is not ready to leave yet and is likely to rebel and run back to the cult, digging deeper inside.

Cults also know nowadays that they can sue family and friends for 'kidnapping' members from their group against 'their will' – can you believe it? That would really 'twist the knife in deeper'! We don't recommend this course of action.

There could be, however, a legal recourse that a family can use that may help their Loved One; at least in the UK, anyway. Since the introduction of **Section 76 of the Serious Crime Act 2015**, which deals with '*Controlling or Coercive Behaviour in an Intimate or Family Relationship*', it might be possible to use this law to prosecute a person or persons in charge of a group, who have controlled or coerced members of that group. As we pointed out in **Stage 4 (page 118)**, there is a direct parallel between how a cult operates, and how an abusive partner controls their spouse (Battered Spouse Syndrome, BSS), so there is a legal argument for using the same laws with a member of a cult, as the 'relationship' mentioned in the Serious Crime Act is not limited to a marriage.

Depending on the situation, sadly, there's often 'intimate relationships' within a cult. It will just be a case of proving it.

The advice given to prosecutors in the **2015 Act** is as follows – "*... a pattern of controlling or coercive behaviour can be well established before a single incident (*of abuse*) is reported. In many cases the conduct might seem innocent – especially if considered in isolation of other incidents – and the victim may not be aware of, or be ready to acknowledge, abusive behaviour. The consideration of the* ***cumulative impact*** *of controlling or coercive behaviour and the pattern of behaviour within the context of the relationship is* ***crucial****.*" - (3.2 Relevant Behaviours).

Does this sound familiar to what is happening to your Loved One within the cult? Yes? Well, it doesn't stop there.

The advice for prosecutors goes on to describe the patterns of this controlling behaviour as, but not limited to, –

- Isolating a person from their friends and family.
- Monitoring their time and actions.
- Taking control over aspects of their everyday life.
- Depriving them access to support services, medical or otherwise.
- Repeatedly putting them down.
- Enforcing rules and activities which humiliate, degrade or dehumanize the victim.
- Taking wages, benefits or allowances.
- Threats to harm them or their children.
- Threats to reveal or publish private information.

Well, if this doesn't describe what happens in a cult, we don't know what does! Please look at the **'Duluth Model of Power and Control'** on **page 119** and make the comparisons for yourself. Try and make a record of all of the actions and examples that support this position. It will be important for when you are building a case.

And it's a case that the police will need to take seriously. The advice that is given by the College of Policing (the professional body for policing in the UK) follows as such, "*The first priority of the police is to make people safe. At domestic abuse incidents it is particularly important that officers take positive action to make the victim and any children safe... Officers must be able to justify the decision* ***not*** *to arrest where the grounds exist and it would be a necessary and proportionate response... If the assessment identifies a risk of harm,* ***it is never appropriate to do nothing****.*" – 'Arrest and other positive approaches', Authorised Professional Practice (APP).

We know that the law is, at the best of times, a quagmire of pitfalls and road blocks, but just imagine if a family (who have the legal right to start an investigation, independent of the victim), were able to win a case against a cult for controlling and coercing their Loved One. It would set a legal precedence for other families to use in the future… nudge, nudge, wink, wink!

But, until that precedence is set, it is sadly true to say that there are no '*Steps and Stages, Levels and Phases*' to get your Loved One out of a cult; the change needs to come from the Loved One. It's frustrating and traumatic. We're very sorry.

There are, however, some things that you can do to change the odds in your favour. These suggestions are no guarantee, but they can help in the long run. There are **8** of them in total… NOT 6… that 'joke' will be lost on you if you haven't read **page 96**!

1) See your Loved One as a victim, not as 'mad or bad'!
This one will be difficult because of your frustrated attempts to make them see how 'stupid' they are being for joining a cult, but it won't help and, in many ways, it isn't fair to judge them in this light. They will have made their decisions with good intentions (wanting to find a better life for themselves and others), but their naïve decision to join a group will have exposed them to systematic techniques of control and manipulation (as we have discussed above), which have been designed to operate undetected. If you can stomach reading **Stage 3** from **page 79**, then you can get an idea of what your Loved One has been subjected to. We appreciate that this may not be easy, as you will probably still have very raw emotions, but please try to ignore the satirical acidity of the book.

Understanding, and reminding yourself on a regular basis, that your Loved One is NOT stupid, crazy or corrupt, but a victim of control, will go a long way to helping you 'bite your tongue' and not saying or doing something that will make things worse. Assuming that you've got any tongue left by now!

2) Don't lose contact with your Loved One.
Again, this one may be very difficult (quite frankly, most of the suggestions are difficult!), as you will have probably got sick and tired of hearing about how amazing the group is from your Loved One. This is assuming that you are allowed any contact at all, not being part of the cult. (Please don't join the cult just to get your Loved One out, as you are putting yourself at a tremendous risk, and it could backfire. If your deception was discovered, you'd be seen as a traitor in the eyes of your Loved One. They would never trust you in the future.)

The point of trying to keep in touch is two-fold. Firstly, you will be countering the narrative that the cult will be forcing onto its members, that people outside of the cult are evil and don't care about their family or friends. If your Loved One sees that this is not true, it might start the process of recognizing the flaws in the ideology of the cult. Secondly, it will remind your Loved One that they are still loved, and that you'll be there for them if they ever change their mind. Those doubts about the veracity of the cult could be 'windows of opportunity' that should be seized upon. They need to know that you will help them through that window, without using the phrase, "I told you so."

Please just read **page 117** for a quick glimpse into the issue.

3) Show unconditional love to your Loved One.

Although this is technically a simple suggestion… in practice, it could REALLY 'stick in the throat' because of the levels of frustration that you'll will be feeling. We are NOT saying love the cult, or love the decisions that your Loved One has made, but tell them that you support them and will always be there for them. As we mentioned, there may come a time when your Loved One secretly questions their choices involving the cult. They will need to know that there is someone who will support them without judgment, as their self-worth will be shot to hell by now, and they will feel incredibly insecure. BE that person. It will be difficult, but BE that person.

So, put on the best smile that you've got, give them a big hug, and through gritted teeth, tell them that you are there for them… even if you just want to smack some sense into them!

4) Try and arrange one-to-one time with your Loved One.

This may be really difficult (Ok, we're going to stop giving this qualifier as it is applicable to most of the suggestions; you get the idea!), as the Cult will always want to 'over-see' any contact that your Loved One will have with 'outside influences'. **But really persist with this one.** Always invite your Loved One to birthday parties, wedding events, anniversary celebrations, public holidays, anything at all that could get you alone with them, so that they can have some breathing space from the unrecognized oppression.

This will again counter the false narrative that family or friends outside of the cult don't care about the Loved One. The key to it though is to NOT TALK ABOUT THE CULT. Just have family fun and a great time. Don't put any pressure on your Loved One.

On a side note, always send a Birthday/Christmas Card to them (and take a photo of each one). They might receive it, but even if they don't, they will at least appreciate later that you always cared.

5) Remind your Loved One of what their life and aspirations were like before they joined the cult.

The cult will have done everything in its power to change your Loved One's view of themselves, and of their hopes and dreams. You need to remind your Loved One of who they were and what they wanted to become as an individual. It will be very tempting, however, to finish it with, "...BEFORE YOU JOINED THAT 'EFFING' CULT!" **Don't do it!** Breathe deeply and resist the temptation; it will just switch them off from your conversation. You need to 'casually' talk about the past, perhaps talking about some relatives or friends that you haven't seen for a while, or passing on some news about someone who they used to know. Perhaps do a spring clean of the house and mention that you've got some of their stuff that you'll be 'holding on to'.

Your Loved One's memories and dreams will be 'in there' somewhere, and just lightly talking about certain things that trigger those memories could be enough to plant a seed of doubt into their minds about the journey that they are on. Lay it on too thick and the defense barriers will slam shut. It will be a difficult balance to get right, but it could be very beneficial.

6) Don't insult or criticize the cult.

We know we said that we wouldn't say this again but... this one will be REALLY difficult... we mean REALLY difficult... but please trust us; don't do it. It will be so counter-productive if you continually criticize the cult. Your Loved One will have been subjected to a serious amount of manipulation, and will no longer see themselves as an individual, rather an integral part of the cult. So, if you insult the cult, your Loved One will see it as an insult to them. They will take it personally and stop listening to you. If you want to get a better idea of this process, then please read **Stage 3: Phase 5: Destroying the Self** from **page 99**, but if it's too painful to do this, then at least read the bottom paragraph on **page 138** to get an idea of what we are talking about.

Once you have expressed your opinion about the cult (try and be as constructive as possible), stop criticizing it; don't call it a 'cult' (as even this will 'trigger' a negative response), and just listen to your Loved One. Get as much information as you can and use phrases like, "*That's very interesting. I don't agree with it, but I love you and I support you.*". Yep! Really, really difficult!

7) Get as much information about the cult as possible.

Even though you shouldn't criticize or insult the cult, there may be occasions when you'll be able to 'lightly' challenge or question both the actions and the ideology of the cult. If you don't have the correct information (perhaps because it's based on gossip or rumour), then your Loved One will reject your position.

Do your research. There may be a group of ex-members of that cult; contact them; they can help you in many ways. Then you might 'strike a chord' when you chat with your Loved One, again, sowing a seed of doubt. Keep sowing seeds. Some may grow.

Another technique is to use **Associative Comparisons**. If you make a critical judgement on their cult, your Loved One will 'switch off' (as they have been trained to do), but if you make a similar judgement on a different group, the same defenses might not kick in, and your Loved One might take on the criticism and then draw their own comparison. It's not a guarantee but it might get another seed to grow.

8) Look after yourself.

It's important to be strong for your Loved One but, as many families of alcoholics and drug addicts will say, it takes a toll on everyone involved. Be good to yourself; get regular therapy; even join groups for ex-cult members; you will be welcomed and supported. If there aren't any in your area, join a support group for families of addicts; they can still help. You will need that support just much as your Loved One will. Be there for yourself. Allow yourself to receive help.

Conclusion

None of this is easy. It is a difficult subject and one that can cause terrible harm to the people involved in so many ways.

We realise that '*Way of the Master*' is not always a 'fun read', and not just because we have a terrible sense of humour! No. It deals with the darker side of human behaviour (the mind of a psychopath is a horrible place to be), and it also continually reflects upon our own flaws and fallibilities that can be used against us; not a nice process for any of us... except for the Epicureans[16].

We hope that the humour has somewhat sugar-coated much of the harder information that needs to be digested, but we understand that it may still leave a bad taste in your mouth. Sorry.

The other 'dark side' to the book is that it acknowledges the messiness of life, with uncertainty and inexact answers for most of our concerns. Wouldn't it be great if there really were simple '*Steps and Stages, Levels and Phases*' to creating a successful life?

But there aren't any. Really sorry.

The difficulty stems from the fact that these fallibilities and ambiguities are an integral part of our beneficial adaptive systems, like pattern recognition, positive projection, virtual mapping and social cognition; there's nothing exact about any of them. It would be tempting to abstain from anything that didn't work perfectly but then we'd be dead within a week. And this is the point. We shouldn't be 'throwing the baby out with the bath water'; we should be improving our ability to know where the dirty water is (**awareness is half the battle**), by developing our Critical Thinking skills, and making appropriate individual decisions for ourselves, rather than being fooled into making a choice that is wrong for us. As we say in the trade – "*You must Train Your Brain to rid Your Life of Strife*" ... OK, we'll stop doing that now!

---

[16] Epicurus (341-270 BCE) was a Greek philosopher who taught that critical reflection, on both the good AND bad aspects of our lives (Parrhesia) is a necessary practice in finding contentment and peace of mind (Ataraxia).

This sounds like a difficult task, but you'd be amazed at how much easier it becomes with a bit of practice. As Prof. Francis said, if the Government introduced Critical Thinking into the national curriculum (as its own subject rather than being part of another, like English Literature), then it would become second nature for everyone, and society, as a whole, would benefit from it (apart from cults… and politicians! Please see the bottom half of **page 156**)

Don't forget, Critical Thinking is not about knowing everything there is to know about an issue; you don't need to have a degree in every subject… or be omniscient! It's about asking some relevant questions about the issue at hand. What independent, verifiable evidence is there for the claims? Could there be ulterior motives for making the claims? Who indirectly benefits from the claims? **Just asking a few extra questions can make all of the difference.**

Don't get us wrong. This won't mean that our lives will become perfect; there is no such thing, but it should improve them greatly.

And, of course, we don't have to critically question every choice that we are going to make in our lives for skepticism to have value; it's not an 'All or Nothing' dynamic (Is that the Binary Landscape of False Dichotomies looming in the distance? Please see **page 70**) No. You're welcome to buy a brand of toothpaste because of how attractive the model is in the advert – ignoring the fact that her teeth have been bleached within an inch of their existence. It's ok.

But when you are going to make life-changing decisions, like choosing a new career or partner, rejecting family and friends… releasing sarin gas onto your local metro system – that sort of thing – then it's imperative that you critically consider your options.

'*Way of the Master*' is, of course, a direct criticism of cults, but it also takes a step back and encourages Skepticism and Critical Thinking for our lives in general. We hope that you can see past the dark satire and welcome the positive ideas found within.

Welcome to your messy, exciting future.

Welcome to… a life that is right for you.

Genuine Author Biographies

John Rico is a criminologist and an author. ***'Blood Makes the Grass Grow Green'*** (2007), his war-time memoir of his tours in Afghanistan, received rave reviews. ***'Border Crosser'*** (2009), his second book about the Mexican border, has rightly received a universal critical drubbing! He lives in the United Kingdom. He considers Scientology to be his arch-nemesis, although, to be honest, the organization is, at present, unaware of this relationship!

Richard Francis is a Train Operator for London Underground. He studied Psychology and Theatre Arts at university… which has really helped him to be a Train Operator for London Underground! His Human Rights activism has led him to collaborate with groups such as 'Humanism UK', 'OneLaw4All' and 'Journey to Justice'. He does have a 'Doctorate in Science'… which he downloaded for free from the Internet.

ACKNOWLEDGMENTS

Genuine thanks go to the following for their ideas, help, and inspiration. Arthur, Valerie, and Andrew Francis, Stephen Fry, Prof. A C Grayling, Louis Theroux, Prof. V S Ramachandran, Maryam Namazie, Janette Smith, Carrie Supple, Will Essilfie, Helen Young, Lauren Vinn, Prof. Bruce Hood, Dr. Michael Shermer, Dr. Ben Goldacre, Prof. Richard Wiseman and, above all, Natasha Nolan.

Book Recommendations

Towards The Light – Prof. A C Grayling

Brainwashing – Kathleen Taylor

Terror, Love and Brainwashing – Alexandria Stein

Supersense, The Self Illusion – Prof. Bruce Hood

Critical Thinking Skills – Stella Cottrell

The Believing Brain, Science Friction – Dr. Michael Shermer

Bad Science – Dr. Ben Goldacre

The Tell-Tale Brain – Prof. V S Ramachandra

The Art of Thinking Clearly – Rolf Dobelli

59 Seconds: Think a little, Change a lot – Prof. R Wiseman

Printed in Great Britain
by Amazon

18090318R00113